Contents

AF798668

Preface

THE REPUTATION of Finger Lakes wines is changing rapidly. Even a decade ago, the Finger Lakes was looked upon by wine writers and wine aficionados worldwide as a place that had decent Riesling, but that was about it. How things have changed. Today the Finger Lakes produces Riesling that competes favorably with the best in the world. The region is looked upon as a leading producer of cool-climate wines in general. And our red wines, which had been either thin and acidic, or flabby and grapy, are now being produced with true character and depth.

This rapid change has been brought on by many things. The Finger Lakes wine world has been fortunate to have had a select group of talented, committed pioneers who believed in the region and knew that world-class wines could be made here. As they began to succeed, the wine media began to take a serious look at the Finger Lakes and saw that something interesting was happening. As a result, the bar of success crept just a bit higher, and higher still with each new accomplishment. These pioneers are cultivating a new generation of dynamic young winemakers and grape growers who are making wines of a quality that would have been unthinkable just a generation ago.

Perhaps most important of all is the unique spirit of camaraderie that flows among the people who grow grapes and make wine in the Finger Lakes. These people are friends, not competitors. They are generous of spirit, generous with their time and expertise, focused on not only making their own wineries flourish but also recognizing that for anyone to succeed here, the region as a whole must succeed first.

This book will survey only the surface level of this region's wines and winemaking. Growing wine grapes, and making wine, is an endlessly complex, detailed process. I cannot pretend to be an expert on wine or winemaking, just someone who enjoys wine and has developed a deep affection for the Finger Lakes and an enduring respect for the people who make wine here. You will not find in this book any guidance on where the "best" Riesling or Chardonnay or Cabernet Franc, or any other wine, might be found, for two reasons. First, the vagaries of weather, winemaking techniques, and a hundred other factors might mean an average wine one year, and a wonderful wine the next, at any given winery. Second, and more important, is that unless you are qualified to be a judge at a wine competition (and I am certainly not), the "best" wine is the wine you enjoy the most. We're all familiar with the French saying, *Chacun à son goût.* This phrase is often translated casually as "To each his own," but that doesn't capture the real spirit; it literally means, "Each person has their own taste." What this means in a wine context is that each individual has to judge whether a wine is pleasing to their palate or not. No one else can tell you what you like.

So this book will not try to tell you what to drink and what not. What it will do is tell you which wineries specialize in a particular wine. It will take note of particular successes they've had in the past, and in general try to steer you through the complex and dynamic Finger Lakes wine world. We will look briefly at the history of wine in the Finger Lakes, which could easily deserve a book unto itself. We'll look at the grapes that grow here, and the wines we make, some of which are unfamiliar to many wine lovers, and why. And the core of the book surveys over fifty different wineries in the Finger Lakes, in each case telling a bit about their story, where and how they source their grapes, and the wines they make. The world of Finger Lakes wines is ever changing and endlessly interesting. Enjoy the journey.

Acknowledgments

WRITING A BOOK like this one would have been impossible without the help of a great many people. Many of them were stationed in tasting rooms throughout the Finger Lakes, and all were invariably friendly and interested in this project and more than willing to answer my sometimes arcane or oddball questions. Thanks go to Brandy Ahouse, Jim Alsina, Janice Brunner, Michael Cecere, Stephen Chamot, Jennie Cook, Erin Flynn, Amanda Gumtow, Dana Hession, Janice Hyde, Jamie Kelly, Russ Nalley, Laura Phillips, Matthew Roseler, Ryan Scammon, Tammy Tones, and Danielle Van Gheem.

Thanks too to the following who spent time with me, in person and sometimes by email, and filled me in with often vital information: Kim Aliperti, Debra Bermingham, Frédéric Bouché, Mario Del Rosso, Jeff Dill, Jim Doolittle, Morten Hallgren, Paul King, Katey Larwood, Liz Leidenfrost, John Leidenfrost, Jr., Kris Mathewson, Bruce Murray, Mike Oleksyn, Tom Prejean, Johannes Reinhardt, Katie Roisen, Liz Stamp, Rob Thomas, and Ryan William.

Very special thanks to Roger Battistella and Hermann Wiemer, both of whom were most generous with their time. And especially to Ken Birman, who has been an extraordinary friend to me and to this project.

Most of all to Sherry Burford, who gave valuable critiques of early drafts of the manuscript, was unfailingly patient and supportive as I wrote this book, and was my frequent partner on wine-tasting visits—taking much better notes than mine.

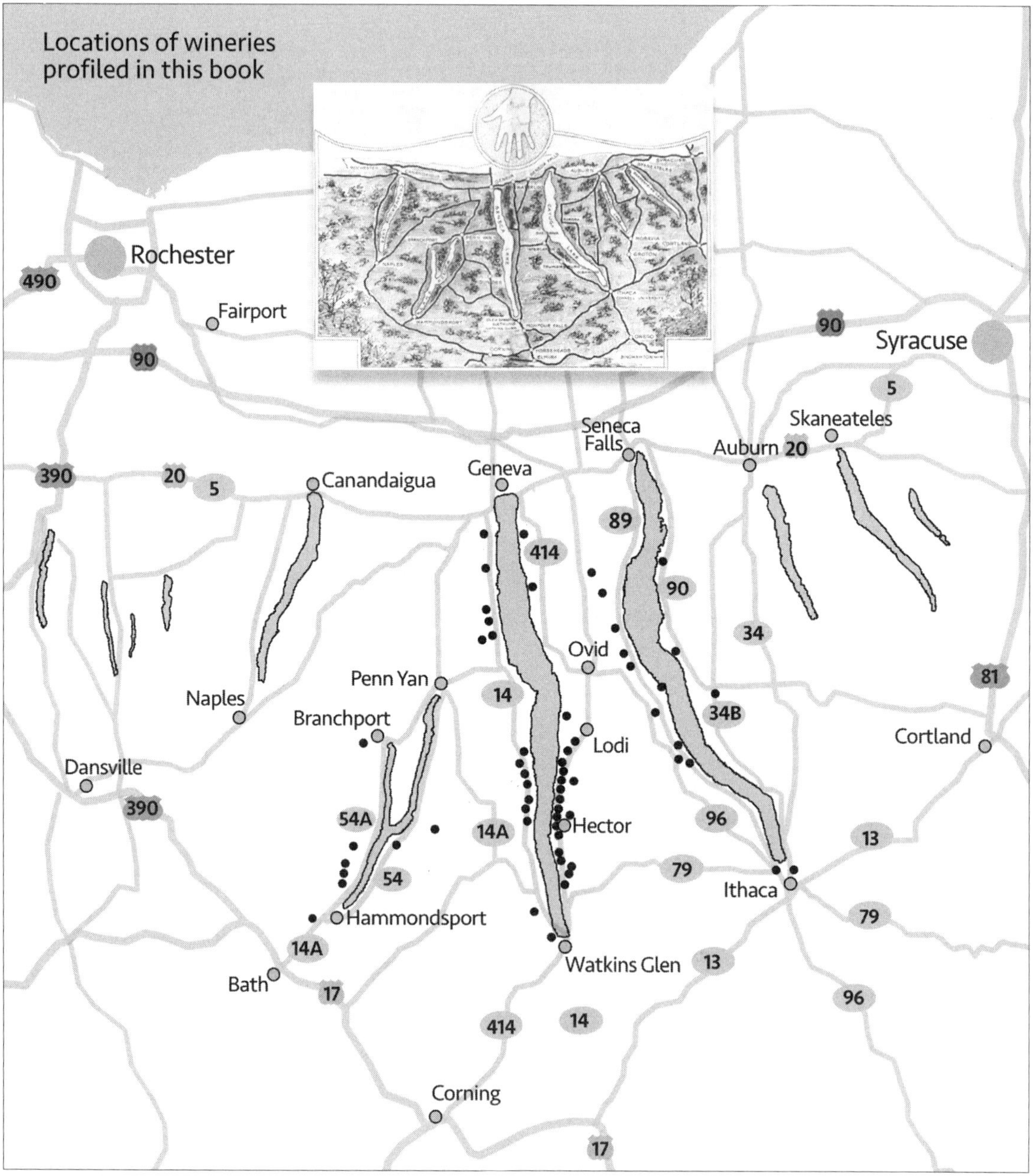
Locations of wineries profiled in this book
Rochester
490
Fairport
90
Syracuse
5
Seneca Falls
Skaneateles
Auburn
20
390
20
5
Canandaigua
Geneva
89
414
90
34
Ovid
Penn Yan
14
Naples
Branchport
34B
Lodi
Cortland
81
Dansville
390
54A
14A
Hector
96
13
79
54
Ithaca
Hammondsport
79
14A
Watkins Glen
13
Bath
17
96
414
14
Corning
17

Introduction

THE ANCIENT IROQUOIS legend has it that the Great Spirit, asked to point to the most beautiful place on Earth, set hands on the ground just south of what would be Lake Ontario. As the fingers drew away, the imprints filled with water and formed the Finger Lakes. None can prove that this was not the case, and many who come here, or live here, find it the most satisfying explanation for these unusual long, deep lakes, eleven in all, radiating roughly north to south.

The scientific explanation holds that over a hundred thousand years ago, much of the northern half of the United States was covered in glacial ice that came and went in a turbulent mixture of water, ice, stone, and soil. Around twelve thousand years ago the ice began to melt for good, and the glaciers to recede northward. As they did so they carved channels in the land, which became rivers flowing north from what is now New York's southern border with Pennsylvania, into what we know as Lake Ontario. Many of these long, deep rivers eventually silted up in places, forming the lakes we call the Finger Lakes.

Like these ancient rivers, the Finger Lakes flow north, very slowly (the lone exception is the western branch of the Y-shaped Keuka Lake, which flows south and then north), eventually flowing into other waterways and then into Lake Ontario, the St. Lawrence River, and finally the Atlantic. Although not as vast as they were in prehistoric times, some of the Finger Lakes are exceptionally deep, with the deepest, Seneca

Lake, at a depth of just over six hundred feet. Second to Seneca in depth is Cayuga Lake, at just over four hundred feet. The lakes, their sloping shorelines, and the rocky, glacier-carved soil are all key pieces of the puzzle that makes the Finger Lakes one of the most interesting and unusual wine-producing areas in the world.

The Lake Effect

Without the lakes, no one could or would grow wine grapes here, for the simple reason that the winters are far too cold. The average temperature in winter in the Finger Lakes is about twenty-six degrees Fahrenheit; in Bordeaux, to take one example, the average is above forty degrees. This would be an unfortunate circumstance, because the soil in the region, dominated by a rich mix of shale, limestone, and loam, is ideal for many types of grapevines. But to the rescue come the lakes.

Water retains temperature much longer than air, and the greater the volume of water, the longer it will take to cool down or heat up to approach the temperature of the air around it. A drop of water outside on a cold winter day will freeze rather quickly; a glass of water will take longer, and a bathtub-full even longer. So it is with the lakes, and this is one of the key reasons why Finger Lakes wines exist. Most of the vineyards in the region sit on land that slopes down toward the lakeshores. Imagine it is January, and the air temperature several miles away is ten degrees Fahrenheit. Closer to the lake the air will be warmer, because the vast volume of water in say, Seneca Lake, over thirty miles long and more than six hundred feet deep, has retained the warmth of the summer and autumn just passed. The vines may be cold, but not as cold as they would be without the lake. With this lake-effect warmth, grapevines for quality wine can survive. Without it they would die.

Almost as important to the grapevines is the nature of the soil. Examine the soil in virtually any region famous for its vineyards and what you'll find is rocks. Lots of them. Whether it's Burgundy, Bordeaux,

Chianti, or the Mosel, vineyards are found in rocky soil. The Finger Lakes region, thanks in part to the roiling of glaciers over thousands of years, has rocky soil in abundance, mostly shale, limestone, and slate. The soil around Cayuga and Seneca Lakes, with what is called calcareous shale (meaning it contains lime and is alkaline), is particularly good for grapevines, which in part explains why so many wineries and vineyards cluster around these lakes.

Another characteristic common to both the Finger Lakes and the famed vineyard regions of Europe and elsewhere is sloping ground. Grapevines do well on a slope because, among other reasons, more sunlight can reach the vines when grown on sloping ground rather than flat, much as staggered seating in a theater makes it easier to see over the head of the person in front of you. To varying degrees, all the terrain approaching the lakes slopes downward, and this is where you'll find most of the Finger Lakes vineyards.

The lakes and their sloping ground also help the vines in both winter and summer by stimulating airflow. Moving air is good for just about all plants, but especially for grapevines. In winter the cold air flows down toward the lakes, rather than collecting or pooling in a single place. This air is warmed by the heat retained in the lake water, and

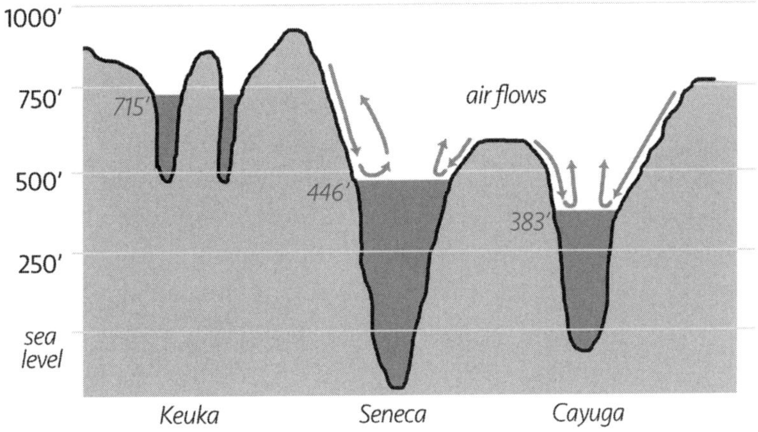

The "lake effect." In winter, cold air flows down the sloping vineyards toward the lake, which retains warmth from the prior months due to the large volume of water. The air is warmed and rises, allowing more cold air to flow downward again. In spring, the lakes retain the cold of winter, delaying bud break until after freezing danger has passed.

it rises back into the vineyard to warm the vines. In spring the lakes are cooler than the air, and this cooling keeps temperatures lower in the vineyards, delaying what is called bud break. If the buds open too soon in spring, the all-too-common plunge in temperature could wreak havoc on the productivity of the vine for that year. The lakes' cooling effect helps to delay bud break until the more reliably warm weather later in the spring.

Geneva Agricultural Experiment Station

Another important player in the Finger Lakes wine world is the presence of Cornell University and the New York State Agricultural Experiment Station in Geneva, at the northern tip of Seneca Lake. Cornell is a land-grant university, which resulted from an act of Congress in 1862 to provide, in each state, at least one college that would be dedicated to research in agriculture. Cornell's founder, Ezra Cornell, took this opportunity to open his namesake university in Ithaca. Since its founding, Cornell has been among other things a leading agricultural research institution focusing mostly on the agriculture of New York State, including dairy farming, apple and fruit orchards, corn and other food crops—and wine grapes. The agricultural experiment station, founded by New York State in 1880, came under the Cornell umbrella in 1923. The station has been and remains the key location for research into wine grapes, and researchers at Cornell and the station have developed new grape varieties and vineyard-management techniques specifically gauged to help grow wine grapes in the Finger Lakes and elsewhere in the state. One of these varieties, Traminette—as implied by the name a grape derived from Gewürztraminer—is a grape developed by plant scientists at the station and is relatively common now among Finger Lakes winery offerings. New varieties that are sometimes encountered include Aromella and Arandell, joining now-familiar station innovations that include Cayuga White (introduced in 1972), Valvin Muscat, and

Noiret (both released in 2006). Station plant researchers are continuously working on new projects with a goal of developing grapes that produce well, are relatively cold-hardy, are naturally resistant to plant diseases, and of course yield a good wine. The station also offers new vineyards an extensive site evaluation to help identify locations with ideal soil, drainage, water availability, and other factors.

Wines of the Finger Lakes

With few exceptions the wines of the Finger Lakes are what is called in the wine world cool-climate wines. Cool-climate wines are those that, naturally enough, are produced in cooler latitudes and areas than other wines. Well-known cool-climate wine-producing areas include Germany (famous for its Rieslings), Alsace, the Champagne region of France, parts of New Zealand, and many others—including the Finger Lakes. Due to both the nature of the grapes grown in cooler latitudes as well as the effect of cool temperatures on the grapes and the wine they produce, cool-climate wines are characterized among other things by acidity, crispness, lower alcohol levels, and minerality. They tend as a result to be very food-friendly wines, a happy coincidence in the Finger Lakes—which, as any resident or visitor knows, can be a food lover's paradise. The cool-climate wine grapes are familiar names in the Finger Lakes: Riesling, Gewürztraminer, Chardonnay, Cabernet Franc, Lemberger, and Pinot Noir, among many others.

Most Americans today would be surprised to learn that in the late nineteenth century the Finger Lakes was the second largest producer of wine in the United States (trailing only California), and by the late 1940s it produced more sparkling wine than did California. As we will see in the next chapter on the history of winemaking in the region, Finger Lakes wines had their beginnings in the mid-nineteenth century and had become a large part of the local economy right up to Prohibition. Gold Seal, Great Western, Taylor, and other wineries were household names throughout the United States, and all were located here. These were very different businesses, and very different wines, from the bulk of the wines produced today by a multitude of small wineries. But winemaking in the Finger Lakes has a storied history.

Reading a Finger Lakes Wine Label

The label will of course tell you a lot about what's inside a bottle of wine, although the only definitive way to know if you'll like it is to open it and have a taste. Still, reading the label carefully first can steer you toward a wine you're likely to enjoy. Here's what's on a typical label here in the Finger Lakes:

1. The name of the winery. Fairly self-evident, and pretty much universal. The only exception that comes immediately to mind is Dr. Frank's "second" label, Salmon Run. Also Tierce, a collaborative project among three wineries (discussed later in this book), bears no single winery name.
2. The name of the wine. This is often the name of the grape or principal grape used in making the wine—Chardonnay, Riesling, Cabernet Franc, and so forth. At other times the name of the wine will be one unique to the winery and designates a blend—Shalestone's Lemberghini, Six Mile Creek's Quintessence, and Atwater's Riewürz would all be examples.
3. The AVA, or American Viticultural Area. This will be either Finger Lakes, Seneca Lake, or Cayuga Lake—the three AVA designations at present

in the Finger Lakes. First, a word about AVAs. The Bureau of Alcohol, Tobacco, Firearms and Explosives, oddly enough, is responsible for overseeing the rules by which wine is produced in the United States, and promulgates these AVA designations as a way to foster community between wine producers and consumers. The goal is to honor a particular area that has carved out a unique wine identity. Exactly what that identity is in the Finger Lakes varies by grape and wine type. An AVA designation means that not only was the wine produced in the Finger Lakes, but the grapes used to make the wine were grown in the Finger Lakes AVA region as well. The Finger Lakes AVA carves out a wobbly oval beginning near Ithaca, through Cortland and up Route 81 to Lafayette, west all the way to Rochester, south to Geneseo, then east back where it began. The region of course encompasses all eleven of the Finger Lakes, although as we will see virtually all the winemaking occurs nearby, or along the shores of, Keuka, Seneca, and Cayuga Lakes. The Cayuga Lake and Seneca Lake AVAs are similar areas, with similar restrictions, for these lakes. Again, to be labeled "Cayuga Lake" the wine must be produced in, and the grapes sourced from, the Cayuga Lake AVA. One has to take AVA designations with hefty grains of salt, however, as they do not carry any guarantee that the wine is good or any better than other wine.

The AVA sourcing rules can also be relaxed, by official dictate, in years when weather conditions deplete the grape harvest to such an extent that fruit needs to be sourced outside a particular region. This occurs very rarely, as the region's vineyardists are experts at combating bad weather and harsh winters, but even they cannot overcome Nature sometimes.

4. The vintage year. This will be the year the grapes were harvested, somewhere between September and November for most wines. Wines can and do age, sometimes for years after harvest and pressing, so the vintage date can be a year or two (or more) prior to a wine's

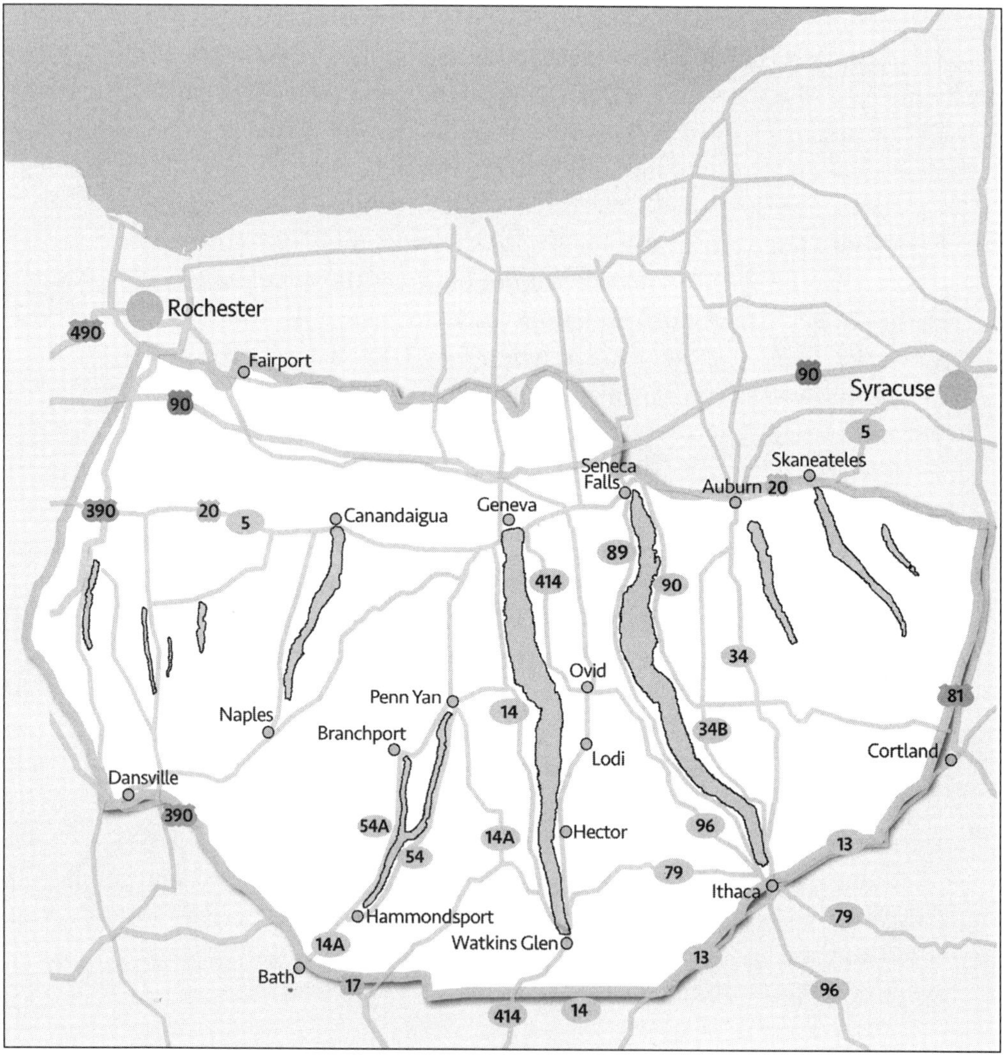

The Finger Lakes AVA (American Viticultural Area)

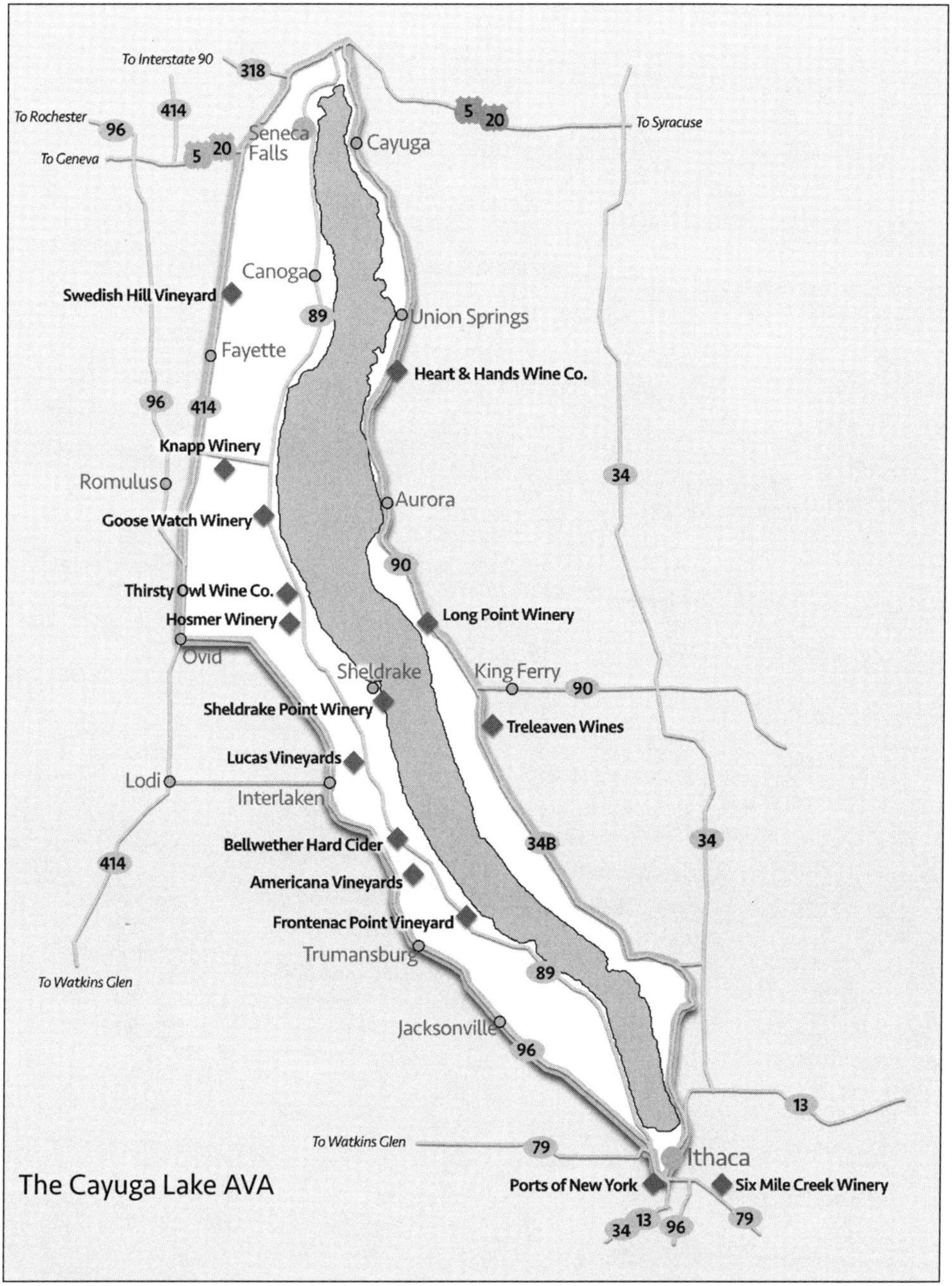
To Interstate 90
318
414
To Rochester
96
To Geneva
5
20
Seneca Falls
Cayuga
5
20
To Syracuse
Canoga
Swedish Hill Vineyard
89
Union Springs
Fayette
Heart & Hands Wine Co.
96
414
Knapp Winery
Romulus
34
Aurora
Goose Watch Winery
90
Thirsty Owl Wine Co.
Hosmer Winery
Long Point Winery
Ovid
Sheldrake
King Ferry
90
Sheldrake Point Winery
Treleaven Wines
Lucas Vineyards
Lodi
Interlaken
Bellwether Hard Cider
34B
34
414
Americana Vineyards
Frontenac Point Vineyard
Trumansburg
89
To Watkins Glen
Jacksonville
96
13
To Watkins Glen
79
Ithaca
The Cayuga Lake AVA
Ports of New York
Six Mile Creek Winery
34
13
96
79

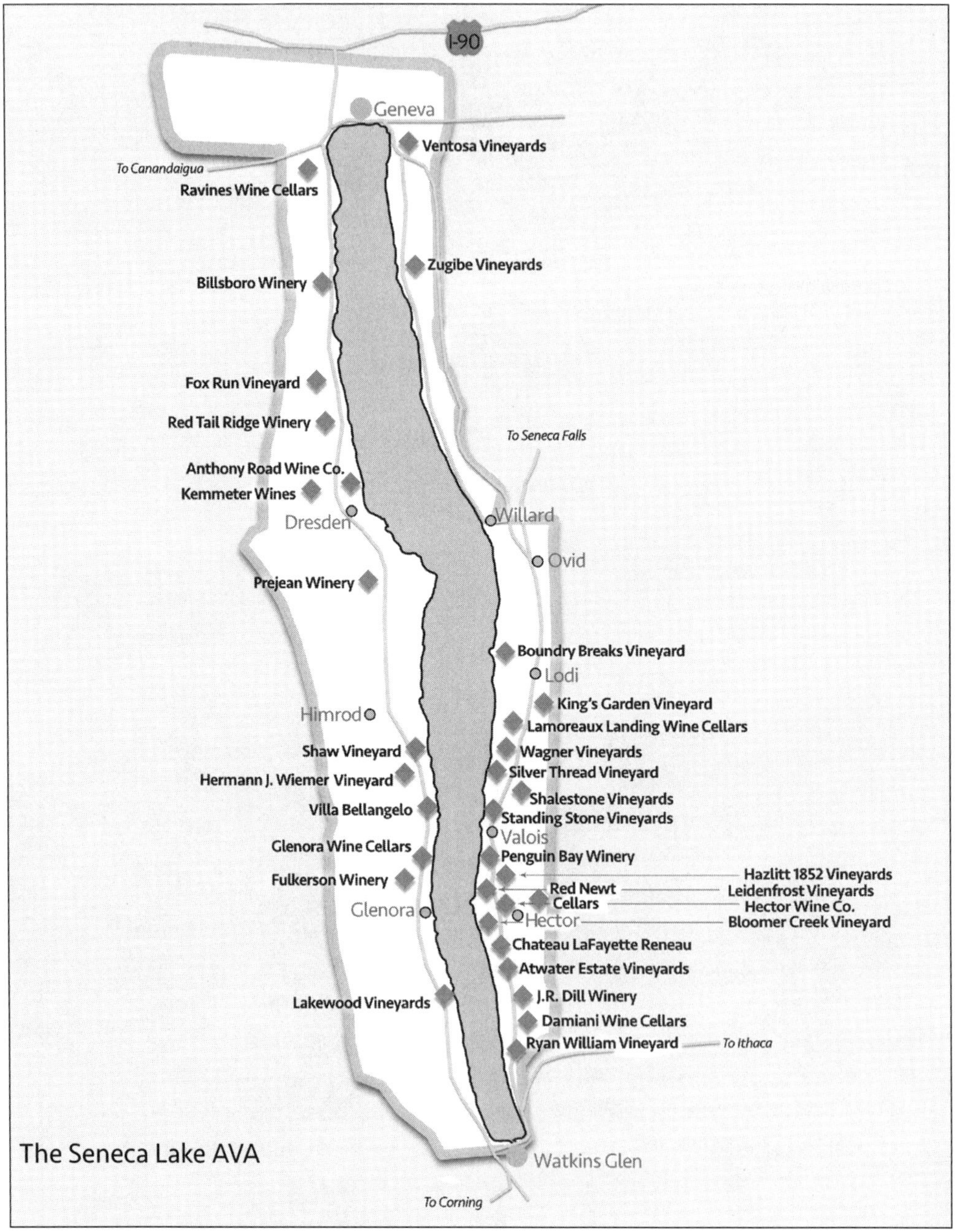
I-90
Geneva
Ventosa Vineyards
To Canandaigua
Ravines Wine Cellars
Zugibe Vineyards
Billsboro Winery
Fox Run Vineyard
Red Tail Ridge Winery
To Seneca Falls
Anthony Road Wine Co.
Kemmeter Wines
Dresden
Willard
Ovid
Prejean Winery
Boundry Breaks Vineyard
Lodi
King's Garden Vineyard
Himrod
Lamoreaux Landing Wine Cellars
Shaw Vineyard
Wagner Vineyards
Hermann J. Wiemer Vineyard
Silver Thread Vineyard
Shalestone Vineyards
Villa Bellangelo
Standing Stone Vineyards
Valois
Glenora Wine Cellars
Penguin Bay Winery
Fulkerson Winery
Hazlitt 1852 Vineyards
Red Newt Cellars
Leidenfrost Vineyards
Hector Wine Co.
Glenora
Hector
Bloomer Creek Vineyard
Chateau LaFayette Reneau
Atwater Estate Vineyards
J.R. Dill Winery
Lakewood Vineyards
Damiani Wine Cellars
Ryan William Vineyard
To Ithaca
The Seneca Lake AVA
Watkins Glen
To Corning

market release. If no vintage year appears, then the wine may be a blend of different vintages. This doesn't necessarily mean inferior wine, but most consumers will want to know the vintage year of a wine to determine its quality (some years are better or worse than others, due to weather conditions) and aging potential.

5. Other label designations that can appear, but don't always, include phrases like *estate grown*, which means the grapes used to make the wine came entirely from the winery's own vineyards. As we will see, many wineries have their own vineyards and make their wine from their own grapes. Other excellent wineries have no vineyards of their own at all. Another phrase that might appear would be some indicator of a particular winemaking process used, such as *barrel fermented*, meaning the wine was fermented in an oak barrel rather than in (or in addition to) stainless steel. This doesn't by itself tell you anything about the quality of the wine, just how it was made. Yet another example would be *méthode champenoise*, meaning "in the method of Champagne," which indicates the wine, sparkling by definition in this case, was made with certain prescribed methods, including in-bottle fermentation.

6. The front of the label often, but not always, includes the level of alcohol, indicated as a percentage of total volume. Most wines in the Finger Lakes tend toward the cool-climate mode of relatively low alcoholic content, which makes them fresher and better suited to accompany most foods. It is always a good idea to check the alcohol percentage of any wine, as this is one good indicator of the character of the wine inside. A Finger Lakes Riesling, for example, might run in the 10 to 12 percent alcohol range; a Cabernet Franc might be 12 or 13 percent. Many wines from California and elsewhere, mostly reds but also whites like Chardonnays, can have alcohol levels at 14 percent or more. These will be big, in-your-face wines, and many palates love them. But a wine at 14 percent alcohol will have a very, very different feel from one at 12 percent, even though it might

seem a minor step, and if you don't care for these wines the label can warn you off. *Caveat emptor.*

Beyond the lakes, the soil, the climate, the heritage of grape growing in the region, and the ongoing research into new grape varieties, the wines of the Finger Lakes that we enjoy today owe their existence primarily to the people who grow the grapes and make the wine. Anyone who spends time in the area is quickly struck by the intriguing variety of personalities that live here, many of whom have arrived in recent years. Attracted by the natural beauty of the area and the respite from the density of cities, the people of the Finger Lakes tend toward creativity, self-reliance, and a mutual love for the land, all essential qualities for assuming the responsibilities of making fine wine.

What makes a Finger Lakes wine? As mentioned above, the wines here have the cool-climate complexion of freshness, acidity, fruit, and minerality, the latter a term hard to describe but a quality that makes the wine more flavor-faceted in general—one of those characteristics one knows when it's tasted. They go well with food, preferably food from the Finger Lakes itself, which is famous for cheeses, meats, fruits, and vegetables grown—many organically—in small farms tended personally by the farmers who will sell you their bounty and are pleased to talk about their land, their animals, and the region they love. The wines are often made in small lots, with astonishing care and attention, by vineyardists and winemakers who are constantly experimenting, creating, learning, and refining the very definition of Finger Lakes wine. And they seem to go exceptionally well with a summer evening at sunset, the brilliant orange-and-red sky reflected on the surface of any one of the Finger Lakes, which have blessed us with such superlative wines.

PART I
The Past: Winemaking Comes to the Finger Lakes

First Beginnings

Picture a sunny day in the quintessential Finger Lakes town of Hammondsport, at the southern end of Keuka Lake. It is springtime, 1829, and down the main street in horse and carriage comes a young man named William P. Bostwick. Hammondsport in 1829 is a rural backwater, with a population of a few hundred souls; surrounding the lake the hills are planted in crops. The townspeople take pride in their little village. There remains one significant gap in village life for many, though, and young Bostwick is here to fill it—he is a clergyman, here to start up an Episcopal church. But the enterprising young churchman is important to us today for a very different reason. Although he did not know it, he was the first of many people to play an important role in bringing wine to the Finger Lakes.

Bostwick was a graduate of Hobart College in Geneva, at the northern tip of Seneca Lake, so he knew the Finger Lakes, and had recently completed his religious education at an Episcopal seminary in Connecticut. He was bent on spreading the word of God to the people here, organizing parishes in Penn Yan and Bath as well as Hammondsport. But it was Hammondsport where he took up residence and became rector of the new St. James's Episcopal Church.

Hammondsport near the turn of the 20th century. Now almost 70 years since Reverend Bostwick, Hammondsport is still surrounded by farmland.

As he set about ministering to the faithful in Hammondsport, Bostwick soon hit upon a logistical problem. There was no convenient source of sacramental wine anywhere nearby. But Bostwick was an enterprising man, and he had a plan. Why not make wine here?

Soon he was planting Catawba and Isabella grapes, and promoting their use in winemaking. His "vineyard" was in a leased plot of land somewhere in the village, probably at the corner of Liberty and Mechanic Streets, and before long sacramental wines were to be had easily. Catawba and Isabella were native to the area, and thus able to withstand the often harsh winters in the Finger Lakes. These native grapes are members of a family known as labrusca grapes, Latin for "wild," and the labruscas have a long and continuing importance in the Finger Lakes wine industry. Countering the labruscas are the so-called vinifera, more properly *Vitis vinifera,* the family of grapes that we typically think of when we talk about wine grapes: Chardonnay, Pinot Noir, Cabernet Sauvignon, Pinot Gris, and so forth. Labruscas are comfortably at home in the Finger Lakes, but vinifera are native to warmer climates in Europe. How this came about takes us back a long, long time before Reverend Bostwick.

The earliest fossilized grapevines date back some two hundred million years, when all the continents were like puzzle pieces collected together in a single landmass that earth scientists have come to call Pangaea. Pangaea was home to many different species of grapes, the wild grapes in one part and the vinifera grapes in another. Without delving too deep into the history of Earth itself, all we need to know is that Pangaea began to fragment, continents formed, and the landmasses we more or less know today took shape and position. As this fragmentation occurred, the European *Vitis vinifera* went one way and the wild varieties went the other, most of them to North America. North America's soil and climate are particularly inviting to non-vinifera *Vitis* varieties, the result of which is that roughly forty-five out of the sixty wild-grape varieties are native to North America.

North Americans had made wine from native grapes for some time, but it was Reverend Bostwick who got things started in the Finger Lakes. (The reverend has some historical competition in another churchman, Samuel Warren, who at the same time was planting the same kinds of vines for the same kinds of reasons in the town of York, in Livingston County, New York. Located just west of the Genessee River, York lies beyond the gravitational pull of the Finger Lakes so far as we are concerned, so we'll stick with Reverend Bostwick as our standard-bearer.) Slowly but surely wine was becoming an industry in the Finger Lakes.

Beginning with the sacramental wines, other growers branched out to make wines for table use.

Producing alcohol for consumption was a significant business in early-nineteenth-century America, but most of it was distilled whiskey. The statistics on whiskey consumption in our young nation are a little appalling, reaching seven and a half gallons per person per year in 1823—note that that's "per person," so the figure will include everyone, babes in arms, fragile elderly ladies, and others unlikely to partake. (By comparison the per-capita consumption of distilled spirits in the United States today is a bit under two gallons per year, averaged over all fifty states.) In the Finger Lakes, the next significant player in our story was a so-called vine dresser, Andrew Reisinger. Reisinger was a German immigrant—the first of many Europeans who would make important contributions to Finger Lakes wines—and it was he who, on his own three-acre vineyard in 1853, began the practice of training and pruning the vines so critical to successful grape growing in the region today.

Shortly afterward, in 1860, the next momentous event occurred, which would launch the history of Finger Lakes wines right through the twentieth century, with the opening of Hammondsport's Pleasant Valley Wine Company. Wine in the Finger Lakes was about to become big business.

Early "Big Four" Wineries

In the nineteenth century and beyond, Finger Lakes winemaking was dominated by four large wineries: Pleasant Valley Wine Company, founded in Hammondsport in 1860; the Urbana Wine Company, founded in 1865, a few miles north of Hammondsport; Taylor Wine Company, founded 1880, in Hammondsport yet again; and Widmer's Wine Cellars, which began in 1888 on Canandaigua Lake in Naples, New York. Of these, only Pleasant Valley survives as an independent winery in the Finger Lakes, but the story of each is often colorful and intriguing.

Pleasant Valley Wine Company

The first of the Big Four wineries, the Pleasant Valley Wine Company opened its doors in 1860, the product of thirteen local businessmen. Pleasant Valley proudly harks back to its heritage as US Bonded Winery #1, meaning it was the first commercial winery officially recognized by the federal tax authorities. Pleasant Valley had a big, early success making champagne-style sparkling wine. A case of it went to one Charles P. Wilder in Boston, a friend of Pleasant Valley president Charles Champlin, who was so impressed with the as-yet-unnamed wine at a dinner party at his club that with raised glass (presumably not his first), he proclaimed, "It is eminently proper to appropriate the entire western continent for its name. I therefore baptize it Great Western." Thus became the rather illogical name for one of the Finger Lakes' most popular early wines, a wine that can still be bought today. Pleasant Valley / Great Western continued to grow through the late nineteenth and early twentieth centuries, survived Prohibition making sacramental wines and everything-but-wine grape products, and was eventually acquired by Taylor in 1961. After bouncing along with the Taylor ownership saga (see below), it was acquired in 1995 by the local Doyle family, which still owns Pleasant Valley.

Taylor Wine Company

In 1880 a cooper (barrel-maker) named Walter Taylor came to Hammondsport, knowing a lot about making barrels but nothing about the wine that might go in them. That had to change when—so the legend goes—one of Taylor's customers paid him in wine, thus opening one of the more interesting chapters in the story of Finger Lakes wine. Taylor's three sons, Fred, Clarence, and Greyton, joined the business prior to Prohibition, and the company grew. During Prohibition, Taylor got by, like its local competitors, making sacramental wine and selling kits of concentrated grape juice to home winemakers, a practice that was legal under the Prohibition laws—even offering house calls to befuddled would-be winemakers who needed to be shown how to make the stuff. The continuing history of Taylor will follow below, as we examine the life and influence of the colorful Walter S. Taylor.

The Taylor Wine Company building as it appears today, where it hosts the Finger Lakes Boating Museum.

Urbana Wine Company

The Town of Urbana extends about four miles north of Hammondsport; there the Urbana Wine Company began in 1865. The name ping-ponged over the years between Urbana and Gold Seal Vineyards, after its signature product, Gold Seal Champagne. After Prohibition, which Urbana survived along with the three other major wineries by making sacramental wines, wine tonics, and miscellaneous grape products, Urbana took the momentous step of hiring Charles Fournier, who came on board in 1934—a step that in many ways ushers in the modern era of Finger Lakes winemaking, as we shall soon see. Urbana / Gold Seal was swept up in the conglomeration of large Finger Lakes wineries that has since become Constellation Brands, and produced its last wine in 1984. (Reportedly new owners of the 1865 building are refurbishing this historic and interesting structure, which is on the National Register of Historic Places.)

The Urbana Wine Company building, just north of Hammondsport, as it appears today . . .

. . . and in the late 19th century.

Widmer's Wine Cellars

The last of our Big Four early Finger Lakes wineries, Widmer's began in 1888, when Swiss immigrant John Jacob Widmer began selling wine to residents of nearby Naples, New York, at the southern end of Canandaigua Lake. Will Widmer, the founder's son, was a student at Geisenheim, Germany's Royal Wine School, and guided the company through Prohibition and beyond. Like the other large wineries, Widmer's changed hands several times and eventually became part of the Constellation Brands family. When Constellation decided to close the winery in 2011 and donate the property to the Rochester Institute of Technology, it seemed like the end of the line for Widmer's. But at the eleventh hour Hazlitt 1852 Vineyards stepped in, bought the winery, and uses it now to produce one of the Finger Lakes "cash-cow" wines, the very popular Catawba-based Red Cat.

Prohibition

These four large Finger Lakes wineries steadily grew their businesses into the early twentieth century, but soon the clouds of the Temperance movement, which had been growing in influence since the late nineteenth century, came to dominate the horizon. Prohibition became law at midnight, January 17, 1920.

The Volstead Act (the act enforcing the Prohibition amendment, the Eighteenth Amendment) prohibited the trafficking or sales of "intoxicating" drink, which it defined as any drink exceeding 0.5 percent alcohol. Important exceptions for the Finger Lakes included one making it legal to produce sacramental wines, which as we've seen had been the genesis of the Finger Lakes wine industry, and a provision that a "head of household" could make up to two hundred gallons per year of "fruit juice" for home consumption. *Fruit juice* was widely interpreted as "homemade wine." It is important to remember that the act did not make consumption, possession, or purchase illegal, only sale or shipment.

The nation was deeply divided over Prohibition. By the mid-1920s it was clear to most people that it was not working. Many concluded that it would be better repealed. The "drys" insisted that it was better to keep a flawed law than to abandon it. Franklin P. Adams, columnist and humorist of the 1920s and '30s and beyond, reflected this back-and-forth in his column in the *New York World:*

Prohibition is an awful flop.
We like it.
It can't stop what it's meant to stop.
We like it.
It's left a trail of graft and slime,
It don't prohibit worth a dime,
It's filled our land with vice and crime.
Nevertheless, we're for it.

Prohibition and the Finger Lakes

Most wineries in the United States, including those in the Finger Lakes, saw no future for themselves with Prohibition as the law of the land and reluctantly chose to close their doors. The Hammondsport Wine Company, at the southern end of Keuka Lake, found itself with three thousand cases of Golden Age Champagne in 1920 that it could not sell, although the company received illegal, but no doubt tempting, offers of $100 per case for the wine, nearly ten times the pre-Prohibition value. Although details remain murky, the company was surreptitiously sold to new stockholders, and the vast storehouse of unsalable champagne shrank to a mere three hundred cases by the summer of 1922. Hammondsport Wine Co. was gone.

Widmer's Wine Cellars was more stubborn. Reconstituting themselves as the Widmer's Grape Products Industry, they produced grape and wine products in impressive variety, always careful to stay within the law. In their own words, on their letterhead, the Prohibition-era

Widmer's made: "Altar wines, wine tonics, wine sauces, mint sauces, wine jellies, mint jellies, fruit jellies, grape jellies, grape syrups, grape pomace, medicinal wines, grape concentrates, de-alcoholized wines, manufacturing wines, rum and brandy jellies, rum and brandy sauces, cider for vinegar stock, manufacturing wine syrups, sweet cider in glass and bulk, crème de menthe wine cordial de-alcoholized." Grape juice, to this day an important product for Finger Lakes grape growers, was Widmer's main product in the 1920s.

The other Big Four wineries—Urbana, Pleasant Valley, and Taylor's—followed a route similar to Widmer's, producing just about anything that could be made from grapes except wine, along with actual wines that fit the convenient loophole of sacramental and medicinal uses. There was in fact no limit on how much sacramental wine a church or synagogue could buy, and not surprisingly they started buying a lot. Physicians also got into the act, commonly prescribing wine for some twenty-seven ailments the AMA had recently (in 1922) "discovered" were helped by regular doses of wine. By the mid- to late 1920s perspicacious observers could see that the long nightmare of Prohibition had at least a good chance of coming to an end, which bolstered the wineries' tenacity. Their reward came on December 5, 1933, when Prohibition was repealed.

We might guess that Prohibition would also sound the knell for vineyards, and many grape growers expected that to be the case. But the happy loophole in the law allowing wine to be made at home meant a surge in demand for winemaking grapes from suddenly enthusiastic home winemakers. Grape prices shot up right after Prohibition began, and in New York grape growers began planting new vineyards at a furious pace. Unfortunately for New York, the California growers saw the same pricing phenomenon, and with their huge acreage and perfect climate they quickly flooded the market. Prices plunged. Although the Prohibition era saw no decline in grape acreage in New York, the profit to be made on the harvest was negligible and the industry withered, rebounding only after the Depression.

For reasons unknown, after Repeal the tastes of American wine drinkers had switched from table wine to fortified wine. It would be forty years before the tide was turned back in favor of table wine, a tide that has since intensified, with fortified wines pretty much an afterthought among American wine drinkers today. But after Repeal the wines of the day were the ports, sherries, "muscatels," and other usually sweet, very alcoholic wines unsuitable for table use.

Shortly after Repeal, in 1934, there arrived the first of the few important individuals whose work made the Finger Lakes wine industry what we know today. His name was Charles Fournier.

Charles Fournier

Charles Fournier, a key pioneer of the Finger Lakes wine industry.

Charles Fournier was the most unlikely person to end up in the Finger Lakes. The highly cultured native of Reims, France, capital of the French champagne world, was by 1926 the chief winemaker at Veuve Clicquot, then as now one of the most prestigious makers of champagne in France. But Fournier's life turned tragic when his wife died in an accident and, perhaps in an effort to begin a new chapter, he accepted a position, for a year's posting at least, as head of the Urbana Wine Company and Gold Seal Vineyards. His entry to the Finger Lakes wine world was full of surprises, and his description of the challenges of winemaking here resonates even today:

> I had no idea of the climate and the grapes I would have to work with. It was a sultry 100 degrees in the shade when I arrived in New York City. Then I tasted Concord, Catawba, Elvira and Isabella wines which, to say the least, gave me a shock. The winter that followed was the third shock! The temperature reached minus-14 degrees Fahrenheit that winter . . . and the following summer 11 inches of rain fell in one night and it took two weeks to reopen the road from Gold Seal to Hammondsport.

Fournier was a visionary, and saw in the Finger Lakes the possibility of sophisticated, world-class winemaking. Turning that vision into reality was considerably more complicated, but it's fair to say that he was the first person of influence in the Finger Lakes wine world who believed that his wines could compete on the world stage. Among his early breakthroughs was his entry to the California State Fair—Charles Fournier New York State Champagne—which won the only gold medal in its class. (The fair promptly closed entry to out-of-state wines thereafter.) But through the 1940s, Fournier was trying many different things in an effort to produce superior wine, including planting vinifera and hybrids. The whole hybrid-versus-vinifera debate has been contentious sometimes, but understanding it is crucial to understanding the world of Finger Lakes wines.

American and French Hybrids

An ***American hybrid,*** such as the Catawba, is a purely American grape; it is a hybrid of (usually) the wild labrusca grapes and some form of vinifera, which occurred in nature at some unknown point in the past. (To make this subject thoroughly confusing, the "American hybrids" are often also referred to as "labruscas.") ***French-American hybrids*** (often shortened to "French hybrids") are the product of human intervention rather than natural happenstance, and their genesis begins in Europe in 1863. Beginning in that year, an ominous phenomenon began to strike vineyards throughout Europe. The vines were dying, and no one could figure out why.

Soon the cause was identified: a root louse, called phylloxera, had arrived from North America sometime prior to 1863 and begun feasting on European vine roots. Curiously the North American vines were resistant to the phylloxera louse and grew quite happily even when the louse was present. But the European vinifera vines were very different, and the phylloxera epidemic would mean the end of vinifera winemaking unless something could be done to stop it.

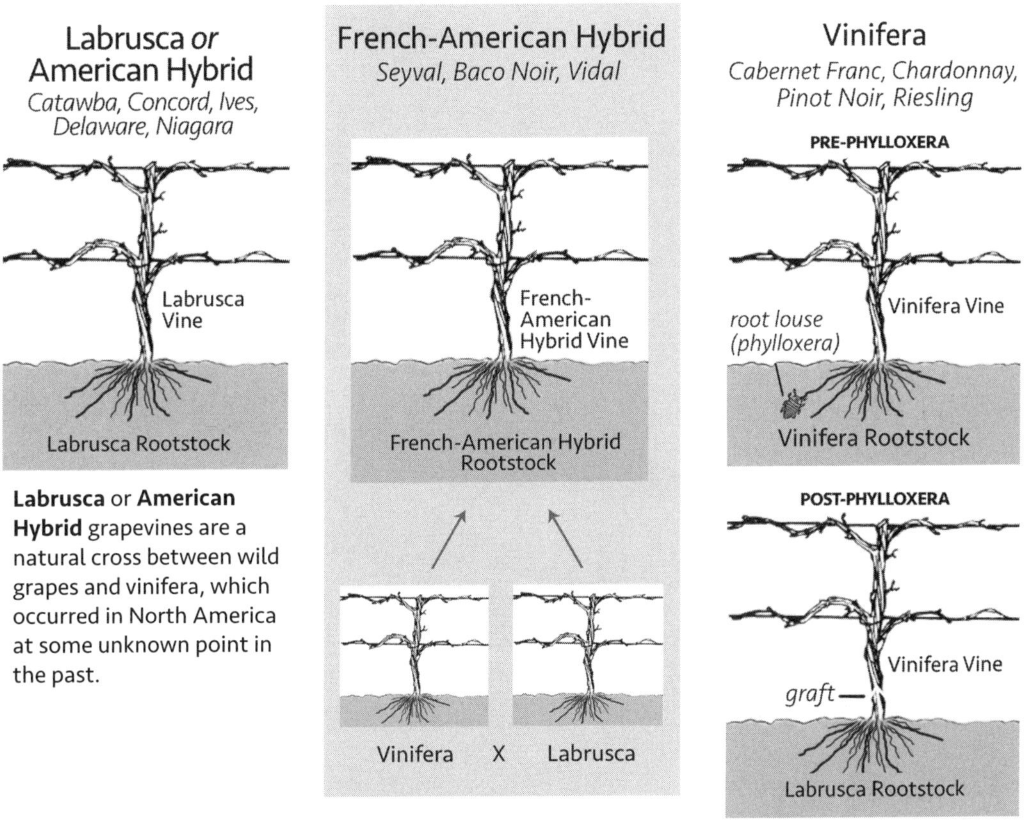

Labrusca or **American Hybrid** grapevines are a natural cross between wild grapes and vinifera, which occurred in North America at some unknown point in the past.

French-American Hybrid grapevines are crosses between the labrusca and vinifera made by plant scientists in the 19th and early 20th centuries. These hybrids were made in an attempt to produce a grapevine that would be resistant to phylloxera. Hybrids are common wines today in the Finger Lakes.

Vinifera grapevines produce the classic wines such as Chardonnay and Cabernet Franc. After the phylloxera epidemic in the late 19th century, vinifera vines were grafted onto labrusca rootstocks. This technique proved effective in defeating phylloxera and today virtually all vinifera grapevines are grafted.

What evolved were two options that proved effective. One was to graft vinifera grape plants onto North American rootstocks, yielding a grapevine whose root was resistant to the phylloxera louse but whose grapes were the same vinifera as before. This option was, in the end, the road taken and indeed, today just about every vinifera grapevine, anywhere in the world, is a graft onto North American rootstocks. The other became the cause of an intrepid group of hybridizers, people who were attempting to end-run the phylloxera scourge by combining a North American grape variety (avoiding labrusca as much as possible due to its "foxy," grapy character) with a vinifera to produce a grapevine that would be resistant to phylloxera. Baco Noir is a good example, produced by François Baco in the early years of the twentieth century and grown commonly in the Finger Lakes. Like all French-American hybrids, its roots and its grapes are pure Baco Noir; nothing has been grafted on to create it.

"Foxy" Wine

Especially in the Finger Lakes, the term *foxy* is a common pejorative used in describing wine. It refers to the grapy, rather cloying quality of wine made from labrusca (wild) grapes, such as Concord or Catawba. The term possibly arises from the fact that wild grapes were sometimes known as fox grapes in early America. Whatever the derivation, a foxy character is not appealing to dry-wine enthusiasts and is generally avoided when trying to produce quality table wine.

While the French hybrids are an important part of the American wine scene, especially in the Finger Lakes, and were widely planted in Europe until the relatively recent past, Europeans tend to take a dim view of the French-American hybrids today, despite the fact that they were developed by creative and industrious Europeans battling to save the (mostly) French wine industry. France outlawed the planting of new hybrids in 1975, in order to protect the vinifera wines.

One of the early advocates of French hybrids in the United States was Philip Wagner, an enthusiastic amateur winemaker from the Baltimore area who did much to promote the use of hybrids in American vineyards.

An avid experimenter and even evangelist for hybrid varieties, he introduced them to Charles Fournier, which in 1944 resulted in the first extensive planting of French hybrids at a commercial American winery. All the Baco Noir, Vidal Blanc, Seyval, and other French hybrid bottlings that have followed in the Finger Lakes owe their existence in a sense to the energy and dedication of Philip Wagner, and the willingness of Charles Fournier to take a chance.

The very first French-American hybrid planted in the Finger Lakes, in the 1930s or early 1940s, was Seibel 1000 (named for hybridizer Albert Seibel), a rosé-wine grape later known as Rosette. Philip Wagner received reports that Widmer's had experienced good success with Rosette, and the success there and elsewhere spurred Wagner to talk up the hybrids as much as he could. His most influential ear was Charles Fournier at Urbana / Gold Seal, who began planting hybrids extensively. By 1946 Wagner arrived for a broad tasting of hybrid-grape wines and was thoroughly impressed, writing, "This tasting represents a turning point . . . on the value of these new varieties." He was of course correct, as the thousands of cases of hybrid wines produced here bear witness. But in the early days, Finger Lakes vintners had to scramble to get vines, most of them obtained through Wagner. It took some years before the hybrids could be grown in significant quantities.

Fournier had also tried planting vinifera varieties, but here the success was sporadic. The climate was too harsh, diseases were difficult to control, and the yields were disappointing. He was not the first to try vinifera. The Agricultural Experiment Station at Geneva, New York, which traces its beginnings back to 1882, was (and remains) one of the principal sources of research and information on grapes in the Finger Lakes region, helping to develop new varieties and to make improvements in agricultural methods. As early as 1902 the Geneva Experiment Station was working on ways to grow vinifera in the Finger Lakes, and published a bulletin on the subject in 1915. Even earlier, Pleasant Valley Wine Co. tried and temporarily succeeded at planting a range of vinifera grapes as early as 1862. But the consensus appeared to be that while intermittent success might be possible, especially with a limited number of vines that could be coddled and kid-gloved, eventually a sufficiently cold winter would come along and wipe out vinifera if planted on anything close to a commercial scale. The challenge seemed too tough, even for Charles Fournier.

A chance meeting at the Geneva Experiment Station would change all that, and dramatically shift the story of Finger Lakes wines.

One gray day in the fall of 1950, Fournier was attending a seminar at the Agricultural Experiment Station in Geneva. During a break between meetings, he later told an interviewer, "I met a man in the hallway who was quite emphatic, and he said 'Why do you not grow vitis vinifera grapes in New York?'" Fournier explained that he had tried, but his interlocutor was suddenly stubborn. "He took me by the lapel and told me he had done it in Russia in a climate similar to New York's and he could do it here."

The man in the hallway was, of course, Dr. Konstantin Frank.

Dr. Konstantin Frank

Frank was born in Ukraine on the Fourth of July, 1899, of German parents. He earned a doctorate in viticulture and agronomy from the Odessa Polytechnic Institute (his dissertation was tellingly titled "Protection of Grapes from Freezing Damage") and entered a successful career in vineyards in the Soviet Union. World War II brought his viticulture career there to an end, and with the end of the war, anti-German attitudes forced the Franks to move to Austria. At age fifty-two Konstantin Frank was ready for a new start, and this Ukrainian immigrant with virtually no English headed for the United States.

The beginnings were challenging. His first job in New York City was as a busboy. Soon he found an opportunity with the New York State Agricultural Experiment Station in Geneva, New York, at the northern tip of Seneca Lake. There he worked on berry research, all the while telling his colleagues—to the extent they could understand his very broken English—that he had grown vinifera grapes along Russia's Dnieper River—which flows through central Ukraine, through Belarus, and into Russia toward Moscow—and he believed he could grow them in the Finger Lakes as well. Few people paid attention to him, until he met Gold Seal president Charles Fournier in the hallway and launched into his pitch. Fournier listened. At last, someone with the means to experiment with vinifera was willing to give him a chance. Frank was hired as director of research at Gold Seal and set out to prove what he had so long maintained.

Dr. Konstantin Frank, the champion of vinifera in the Finger Lakes.

In Ukraine, Konstantin Frank had developed a new design for a vineyard plow that would cover the vines at their base in autumn with earth and uncover them in spring, which was the effective but always labor-intensive method of enabling grapevines to withstand intense cold. In the Finger Lakes his approach was augmented by careful selection of rootstocks that would survive Finger Lakes winters. Onto these (mostly) *Vitis riparia* rootstocks he grafted vinifera grapes and, over years of experimentation, succeeded far beyond what anyone had previously thought possible. Constant experimentation with rootstocks was required. His industriousness in the early years at Gold Seal is almost unbelievable. In something like six years he grafted 250,000 grapevines. He tried fifty-eight different rootstocks, twelve vinifera varieties, nine soil types. *Relentless* is too soft a word for Dr. Frank. He was a force of nature.

He also hated—not too strong a word—French-American hybrids, maintaining they made inferior wine, and the strength of his emotion on this score led to the end of his relationship with Gold Seal. It was Frank's insistence on the primacy of vinifera grapes, as well as his restless desire to have his own winery, that finally led to the breakup with

Gold Seal. In 1956 Frank had purchased land on the shores of Keuka Lake with the intention of planting vines there, and in fact he made the purchase with considerable assistance from Charles Fournier, who was hoping that Frank would continue on as a Gold Seal consultant while getting his new winery up to speed. But by the early 1960s new ownership at Gold Seal was calling the shots above the head of Fournier, and Dr. Frank and the new owners were headed for a collision. In 1961 Dr. Frank insisted that all the labrusca and hybrid vines at Gold Seal be pulled up and vinifera planted in their stead. Gold Seal management, to the consternation of Fournier, told Frank to pack up and go, which he did and headed off to Keuka Lake's western shore to begin work on Vinifera Wine Cellars in earnest. As Frank put it later, with characteristic truculence, "I left Gold Seal because it was sold to people who showed no interest in me or what I was doing . . . I couldn't change them. I say good-bye. The next day I take a shovel and start digging the winery." This, we will recall, at age sixty-two. Frank was nothing if not determined.

Dr. Frank and Charles Fournier, in the 1970s.

Fournier looked on all this with dismay, mainly because when Dr. Frank shut the door behind him at Gold Seal, along with him went most of the detailed knowledge of successfully planting vinifera in the Finger Lakes. Although Frank and Fournier maintained a cordial relationship thereafter, Frank would never again set foot in the Gold Seal winery.

This moment was a watershed. Frank was interested in top-quality, handcrafted wines. The four main players in Finger Lakes wine—Gold Seal, Taylor, Pleasant Valley, and Widmer—kept their focus on wines that could be sold at high volume. It was a classic breach—wine is of course both an art and a business, and each winery has to make a decision on what part of the spectrum to occupy. Frank headed far to the side of art; the world he left behind was still far to the side of business.

Walter Taylor and Bully Hill

One other winemaker in the area was also interested in quality wine, although he was completely unlike Dr. Frank. Walter S. Taylor, the renegade son of Taylor president Greyton Taylor, had the stubborn head of Dr. Frank combined with the P. T. Barnum heart of a showman and publicist.

One of the most colorful and interesting characters in the history of Finger Lakes wineries, Walter S. Taylor was the heir apparent to lead the Taylor Wine Company. Taylor had its roots in Hammondsport going as far back as 1880, when his grandfather Walter Stephen Taylor founded the company. Taylor's sons Clarence, Fred, and Greyton took it over and steered the company through the Prohibition years, after which it continued to grow. Taylor was the biggest of the Finger Lakes wineries by the 1960s, and bought out Hammondsport rival Pleasant Valley Wine Co. in 1968. Taylor produced native-grape jug wines, including the ubiquitous (and still available) Taylor Lake Country Red and Taylor Lake Country White. This was not the kind of wine the young Walter S. Taylor wanted to make, and he was characteristically vocal about it, maintaining that the large wineries (including Taylor) were adulterating their products with grape juice brought in tank cars from California and other oenological misdeeds. The higher-ups at Taylor

The irrepressible Walter S. Taylor with his goat, Guilt Free.

had heard enough, and in 1970 Walter S. Taylor was shown the door.

Prior to his ouster, in 1967, Walter had set up a new winery, Bully Hill Vineyards. There he produced wines from French-American hybrids and was progressing nicely after the split with his namesake winery. But soon the family association would cause considerable headaches.

In 1976, shortly after the death of Clarence Taylor, the Taylor Wine Company was sold to the Coca-Cola Company, which decided to make Taylor a "national" brand by forming a second Taylor in California, ramping up production with abundant California grapes, and restyling it as Taylor California Cellars. Walter continued on his happy way at Bully Hill but quickly ran into the corporate lawyers at Coca-Cola, which along with the Taylor Wine Company had also acquired the right to use the name Taylor in association with wine. Coca-Cola immediately enjoined Walter from using the Taylor name in connection with any winery, which he had been freely doing at Bully Hill. Not one to roll over, Walter Taylor took his case very publicly to the courts, where he lost (Coca-Cola indeed, the court ruled, had the sole right to the Taylor name in connection with wine), and to the court of public opinion, where he was highly successful. A master of publicity stunts, Taylor would paper over the name Taylor on the signs on his winery and made frequent public appearances with a goat, "Guilt Free," proclaiming, "They took my name, but they cannot get my goat." Guilt Free lives on among the labels of Bully Hill wines today, with wines called Love My Goat and Goat White featuring images of the animal, and bearing labels drawn by Walter S. Taylor himself. (Bully Hill's quirky but appealing label designs retain much of Taylor's upstart personality.) Take a careful look at a Bully Hill label, such as that on Bully Hill's Baco Noir, and you'll find that the name Walter S. appears, followed by a censor's redacting black box. The row with Coca-Cola

The row with Coca-Cola over the use of the Taylor name lives on. "Taylor" has been redacted on this Bully Hill label.

lives on, although Coca-Cola no longer owns the Taylor wine business.

Taylor California Cellars was a successful brand in the world of jug wine, but the wine business was not as appealing to Coca-Cola as the surety of carbonated sugar-water, and Taylor was ping-ponged around the universe of large corporations in the ensuing years, with ownership passing to Seagram's, Vintner's International, and finally Canandaigua Wine Company, now a wine conglomerate called Constellation Brands that lists well-known California labels such as Mondavi, Ravenswood, Simi, and others in their stable of wineries. Taylor today is but a small cog in the Constellation Brands machine, no longer a winery but still a trade name. Bully Hill, however, is still very much in business and one of the most popular stops with visitors on the Wine Trail.

When Walter Taylor was dismissed from Taylor Wine Company and went to ramp up Bully Hill Vineyard in earnest, he needed a good winemaker. To his credit, and perhaps luck, he found one of the Finger Lakes' best, a young man from Germany named Hermann Wiemer.

Hermann J. Wiemer

Hermann J. Wiemer

The Wiemer family had roots in winemaking in the Mosel Valley of Germany going back some three hundred years. Born in 1941, Hermann J. Wiemer grew up in war-ravaged Germany and as a young man studied viticulture and winemaking at prestigious institutions in Germany. He was an especially skilled grafter of vines from practice in his family vineyards, though his ambition for winemaking was tempered by his firsthand knowledge of how hard his family had to work for relatively little return. He wasn't certain that he wanted to go into the wine business. But a chance visit from an American visitor to his professor in Germany gave him an interesting opportunity.

The visit was from a representative of the O-Neh-Dah vineyard on the western side of Hemlock Lake, near Conesus. O-Neh-Dah was, and still is, a leading producer of sacramental wines for the Catholic Church, but their vineyards needed significant work. The winery needed someone who knew vineyards and winemaking. Did the professor know any likely candidates?

Hermann Wiemer took the job and came to the Finger Lakes in 1966. His work at O-Neh-Dah was productive and he loved the area, but with scant English and a remote location in Conesus he kept his tenure there short, returning to Germany after a year. Before he went back, however, he met a man at a party and they talked wines and winemaking. Back in Germany, Hermann soon got a phone call from this casual acquaintance. It was Walter S. Taylor, offering him the job of winemaker at Bully Hill.

Wiemer returned to the States in 1968 and joined Taylor at Bully Hill. What he found was a winery owner who overflowed with ideas and ambitions, but had relatively little knowledge of making quality wine. At Bully Hill the hybrid grapes reigned supreme, and although Wiemer could successfully make a drinkable wine from the hybrids, he felt you had to make real vinifera wine if you were going to get anywhere as a serious winery. Taylor, meanwhile, believed vinifera was too risky and the hybrids made more business sense. This hybrid–vinifera conflict, which echoes the experience of Dr. Frank at Gold Seal, was a constant source of tension and friction between Taylor and Wiemer. Taylor just did not want the vinifera, and Wiemer did not want the hybrids.

By the mid-1970s Hermann knew the friction was becoming overwhelming, and he would have to set off on his own. He found a 130-acre bean farm on land that he felt would work on Seneca Lake, so he bought it and started planting vines there. This land grew to become Hermann J. Wiemer Vineyards, although not without some rough times along the way. Wiemer continued making wine at Bully Hill while cultivating his own winery on Seneca Lake. In 1979 he had produced four barrels of Riesling. He had the idea to label it as "dry" in an effort to get wine writers and the public to be more accepting of Riesling, which at the time still had the Blue Nun / Liebfraumilch stigma of being a sweet, uninspiring wine. This was the first "Dry Riesling."

This first wine was a hit. Terry Robards of the *New York Times* raved about it, even running a photo of Hermann Wiemer in the newspaper. Back at Bully Hill, Taylor was not happy.

Hermann knew his tenure at Bully Hill was almost over. Before he returned to Germany for the holidays in December 1980, Wiemer told his second-in-command to be prepared to take over—that Hermann wouldn't be back. He was right: On December 29 he received a telegram from Walter Taylor, informing him that his employment had been terminated. Like Dr. Frank, and like Taylor himself, Wiemer was now discharged from his job but free to create his own winery in earnest.

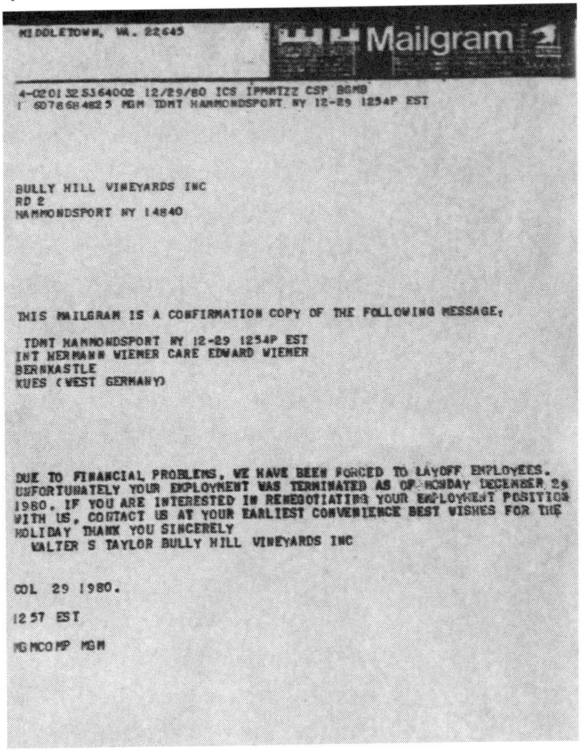

MIDDLETOWN, VA. 22645

Mailgram

4-020132S364002 12/29/80 ICS IPMMTZZ CSP BGMB
1 6078684825 MGM TDMT HAMMONDSPORT NY 12-29 1254P EST

BULLY HILL VINEYARDS INC
RD 2
HAMMONDSPORT NY 14840

THIS MAILGRAM IS A CONFIRMATION COPY OF THE FOLLOWING MESSAGE;

TDMT HAMMONDSPORT NY 12-29 1254P EST
INT HERMANN WIEMER CARE EDWARD WIEMER
BERNKASTLE
KUES (WEST GERMANY)

DUE TO FINANCIAL PROBLEMS, WE HAVE BEEN FORCED TO LAYOFF EMPLOYEES. UNFORTUNATELY YOUR EMPLOYMENT WAS TERMINATED AS OF MONDAY DECEMBER 29 1980. IF YOU ARE INTERESTED IN RENEGOTIATING YOUR EMPLOYMENT POSITION WITH US, CONTACT US AT YOUR EARLIEST CONVENIENCE BEST WISHES FOR THE HOLIDAY THANK YOU SINCERELY
WALTER S TAYLOR BULLY HILL VINEYARDS INC

COL 29 1980.

1257 EST

MGMCOMP MGM

Walter Taylor's famed telegram to Hermann Wiemer. As with Dr. Frank and Taylor himself, a dismissal opened the door to working on the new winery in earnest.

At almost the same time as the telegram from Walter Taylor came news of what is called the Christmas Massacre of 1980. This blast of arctic air came more suddenly and severely than any in memory—the weather went from raining, to fifteen below zero, in something like twenty-four hours. Huge numbers of vines were lost, virtually all were damaged, and vinifera vines took it particularly hard. It was touch and go whether the vinifera were going to make it. Fortunately,

Wiemer had learned from Dr. Frank to cover the grafts with soil in the fall, a practice that most Finger Lakes vineyards employ today. This helped a lot to alleviate the damage. After the Christmas Massacre, Wiemer had some doubts whether vinifera winemaking could be done in the Finger Lakes after all; maybe it really was too hard. He had a tempting offer from Gallo to make wine in the Salinas Valley, but in the end he couldn't see himself there. He came back to the Finger Lakes, and got back to work on HJW Vineyard.

After the Christmas Massacre, Wiemer saw that the vines at one of Taylor's vinifera vineyards had survived the cold rather well. Taylor was struggling by now, so they were open to an offer. Wiemer bought the vineyard, known today as Wiemer's Magdalena Vineyard, and continued on his way with what he knew was prime Finger Lakes vineyard land. (We take up the rest of the Wiemer story on page 164, where we talk about today's Hermann J. Wiemer Vineyard.)

Along with Taylor, the others of what had been the Big Four wineries in the Finger Lakes were falling on hard times, the result of changing tastes and times. Wine was still big business in the Finger Lakes, but it took a hard turn in the jug-wine direction. Taylor had already acquired Pleasant Valley, which by now had been rechristened Great Western, in 1962. But it was the relatively small, unassuming Canandaigua Wine Company that would eventually vacuum up the remnants of the Big Four. Canandaigua Wine Company was a small operation owned by Widmer's when it was sold in 1945 to a keen businessman, Marvin Sands. Sands grew the company steadily, producing inexpensive bulk native-grape wines, until in 1954 the company introduced a product called Richards Wild Irish Rose. This is a sweet, alcoholic, Aurore-based liquid that, let us say, keeps the emphasis on "wild." The success of this product propelled Canandaigua to expansion by acquisition. As noted above it has grown (as Constellation Brands) to include many highly regarded wineries in California and elsewhere.

Canandaigua bought the fading Widmer's in 1986, a case of the child overtaking the parent in a sense, and also acquired Monarch Wine Company, the corporate entity behind Manischewitz. Production of Manischewitz was moved to Widmer's, thus accounting for the rather odd circumstance of the Finger Lakes becoming a major producer of kosher wines.

Kosher Wines

Among the sacramental wines that sustained the Finger Lakes wine industry during Prohibition were kosher wines, which were and continue to be produced in the area. Kosher wine as most Americans know it is a cloying, sweet, rather thick concoction of Concord grapes, and not something a serious wine person would want on the table. Indeed, for sacramental purposes at Jewish religious services typically only the smallest sip of wine does the trick, which is just as well. But kosher wine need not be what we typically encounter. To be kosher, the wine must be produced under rabbinical supervision; it must not come in contact with anything un-kosher (and thus all the equipment used in its production must be dedicated exclusively to kosher wine); the grapes and wine must be handled by Sabbath-observant Jewish males; and no work may be performed on the Sabbath or High Holy Days. Nothing stipulates the kind of grape or level of sweetness. Thus "kosher wine" as we tend to think of it is simply a style of wine, but not the only one. Most good wine shops will stock a number of perfectly decent vinifera-based red and white kosher table wines, especially in the days preceding Passover. These are not (alas) produced in the Finger Lakes, although the area is still home to Manischewitz, one of the most common Concord-based kosher wines, which was produced at the Widmer's Winery in Naples until production was transferred to a Constellation Brands winery in Canandaigua and the Widmer's facility was sold to Hazlitt.

• • •

The demise of the old-line Finger Lakes wineries comes as little surprise to the modern wine consumer who has grown up on a global array of (mostly) vinifera wines. Although the post–World War II consumer had a taste for foxy, native-grape wines, this taste faded through the 1960s and '70s as European wines became more readily available. By the waning years of the twentieth century these wines had only a sliver of the market they once enjoyed. Fortunately for the Finger Lakes wine industry, a new vision had arisen of what Finger Lakes wines could be, a vision spearheaded by the likes of Charles Fournier, Konstantin Frank, Walter Taylor, and Hermann Wiemer. And that, plus one crucial bit of help from the New York State legislature that we will examine now, brings us to the beginnings of the Finger Lakes wineries we know today.

Farm Winery Act of 1976

Other states had passed laws intended to bolster the success of relatively small-scale winemaking, notably Pennsylvania in 1968. The pendulum in consumer tastes was swinging away from bulk wines represented by Taylor's and others, and in favor of quality vinifera and hybrid table wine. Growers of Concord and other native grapes were selling less and less of their product, and the New York wine industry was in serious trouble. The Farm Winery Act was instrumental in lowering the costs and red tape that had made an already tough financial model nearly unworkable.

Passage of New York's Farm Winery Act of 1976 was a watershed moment in the development of the Finger Lakes wine industry we enjoy today. Several planets had to come into alignment to make it happen. To begin, the pressure on New York grape growers was becoming intense, as declining interest in Concord grapes for winemaking led to a steep falloff in sales. People interested in making wines on even a small scale found that the licenses and fees, at least $1,600 per year, were more than they wanted to pay. Restrictions on retail sales at wineries were perhaps the biggest issue, limited under existing law to 5 percent of the gross sales in the prior year. Winery owners, and prospective owners, felt these regulations had stacked the deck against success in an already highly uncertain business.

Enter John S. Dyson, New York State commissioner of the Department of Agriculture and Markets, and the other main "planet" to come into alignment. Dyson was not only an effective legislative operator but also destined to be a winemaker, launching his Millbrook Vineyards in Millbrook, New York, in 1988. Dusting off a farm winery bill that had died on the vine in prior sessions, he and others, notably Lieutenant Governor Mary Ann Krupsak, pushed the act through and Governor Hugh Carey signed it into law in June 1976. New York State was now on the side of small wineries: Promoting New York wines, drastically reducing the fees involved, abolishing the 5 percent cap on retail sales, and other measures suddenly made running a winery a business where talented winemakers could possibly turn a profit.

Glenora and Heron Hill were the first in the Finger Lakes to take advantage of the Farm Winery Act, both opening in 1977, only a year after passage. Hermann J. Weimer Vineyards followed in 1978. Suddenly small-scale, high-quality wineries were becoming a force in the Finger Lakes. It was never going to be easy, but the scene was set for the wineries that we know today.

PART II
Wines, Grapes and Winemaking in the Finger Lakes

1 | *Grapes for Finger Lakes Wine*

THERE ARE THREE distinct species of grapes that go into making Finger Lakes wine. *Vitis vinifera,* or simply vinifera grapes, are the grapes we commonly think of in wine—*Vitis vinifera* is Latin for "wine-making grape." Chardonnay is a vinifera, as are Cabernet Sauvignon, Riesling, Pinot Noir, and so on. There are many, many different varieties of vinifera grapes but, unfortunately for the Finger Lakes, relatively few of them can grow here. The predominant vinifera grapes in our region are Riesling, Chardonnay, Cabernet Franc, and Pinot Noir, but there are many others, some of which are discussed here. Others are rarities: Sangiovese, for example, the grape of Tuscany that is the principal grape in Chianti, is grown in the Finger Lakes (at Ventosa Vineyards and elsewhere) but is not a common Finger Lakes wine.

The second important group of wine grapes are the hybrids. As we've discussed in the prior chapter, hybrid grapes combine two different grape varieties into a new type of grape. There are two subgroupings of hybrids important to Finger Lakes winemaking. The French-American hybrids are the result of work by nineteenth- and early-twentieth-century European scientists who were spurred to find a solution to the phylloxera epidemic that began in the 1860s. These hybridizers include

François Baco, Albert Seibel, Bertille Seyve, Jean Louis Vidal, and many others, whose names live on in grape varieties familiar to many in the Finger Lakes, such as Baco Noir, Vidal Blanc, and Seyval Blanc. The other grouping of hybrids common to the Finger Lakes originate with the New York Agricultural Experiment Station in Geneva. There grape scientists, perhaps the most prominent being Cornell scientist Bruce Reisch, have developed a number of hybrid grape varieties in recent years, including Traminette, Aromella, Noiret, and Valvin Muscat.

François Baco, the developer of Baco Noir. Baco was one of many European plant scientists who developed the French-American hybrid grapevines.

The third group of wine grapes is the original labrusca, or wild, grape varieties. These are not literally wild, although they derive from wild grapes that grow naturally, mostly in northern North America. The labruscas include Concord, Catawba, Niagara, Ives, and others. Labrusca grapes are important to the Finger Lakes wine industry as a whole, and to its history, but they will receive scant attention in this book as they tend to produce overly sweet, uninteresting wines and are almost never a part of the conversation in the world of quality table wine.

Vinifera Grapes

CABERNET FRANC

Although not as commonly known as the other "Cab"—Sauvignon—odds are good that any wine lover has had Cab Franc if they've ever sampled a bottle of Bordeaux. Cabernet Franc is one of the main grapes blended (typically with Cabernet Sauvignon and Merlot) to produce the famed Bordeaux of France.

Cabernet Franc is a bit more cold-tolerant than Cabernet Sauvignon, which makes it attractive to Finger Lakes winemakers. Although it may lack a little of the body and deep color of Cabernet Sauvignon, it's still a delicious, three-dimensional wine that pairs well with food. Cab Franc (as we will typically call it here) often has a green-pepper aroma and flavor, which is fine in modest doses but in abundance signals grapes that were harvested too soon—a not uncommon problem in the Finger Lakes, where the weather sometimes works against grape ripening.

Most Finger Lakes winemakers produce Cabernet Franc. Among the vinifera (traditional wine-producing) varieties, Cab Franc ranks third in acres planted, behind Riesling and Chardonnay.

Notable producers of Cabernet Franc include Shalestone (the "all-red" winery), Leidenfrost, Ravines, Standing Stone, and many others. This is probably the most popular among the vinifera red wines produced in the Finger Lakes, and with good reason.

CABERNET SAUVIGNON

Cabernet Sauvignon (or commonly just Cabernet) is one of the most familiar wine grapes for red wine, and indeed this variety is grown all over the world, including the Finger Lakes. The most famous expression of Cabernet is found in the great wines of Bordeaux, where it is blended with Cabernet Franc, Merlot, and sometimes other grapes to produce what are among the most celebrated wines in France. In the United States and elsewhere, Cabernet Sauvignon is usually produced as a varietal, or single-grape wine, where it is extremely popular.

The characteristics of Cabernet Sauvignon change somewhat depending upon the climate in which the grapes are grown. The wine is always tannic and acidic, giving it great aging potential, and in moderate climates produces a beautiful balance of fruit, tannins, "mintiness," and other flavors. Cool-climate cabs often yield a wine with green-pepperish, herbaceous, or cedar notes that can be appealing to many palates but less so to others. Cabernet Sauvignon from any region is usually aged in oak, which tends to round and soften the flavor blend. Alcohol content of Cabernet varies with the climate and the winemaker, from a low of 12.5 percent to wines in the range of 14 percent and even beyond for some California Cabernets.

Finger Lakes Cabs tend naturally toward the cool-climate side, with herbaceous, relatively low-alcohol wines that can be consumed within a year or two of the vintage or put down for aging. While a relatively common red wine in the region, it is far from the top in red-wine production with just over eighty acres planted, probably owing to the difficulty of making a top-drawer Cab in a cool climate.

Many of the major Finger Lakes vineyards produce a Cabernet Sauvignon, but not with every vintage year, waiting for warmer vintages to make the ideal wine. Lamoreaux Landing, Shalestone, Damiani, and King's Garden make dependable, often excellent Cabernets, as do many others.

CHARDONNAY

Chardonnay is perhaps the most familiar white-wine grape in the world, grown in virtually every wine-producing area from Australia to California. It is the grape that makes the finest French Chablis from Burgundy as well as the everyday, casual wines consumed at wine-and-cheese get-togethers all over the world. Chardonnay is a relatively cold-tolerant wine grape and as such has always been popular among Finger Lakes winemakers. Today virtually every winery in the area that produces white wine includes Chardonnay among their offerings. Chardonnay comes in second only to Riesling in acres planted by Finger Lakes grape growers.

Wine lovers tend to fall into two camps when raising a glass of Chardonnay: "To oak, or not to oak," is the question. A mouthful of Chardonnay can seem rich, heavy with vanilla, alcoholic, and decidedly "oaky," a wine that tends to grab you by the lapels and fill up your taste buds with strong flavors. Many California Chardonnays fall into this camp. Or it can be crisper, more acidic, a balance of fruit, light oak, and other flavors, ideally in a complex balance that demands attention in more subtle fashion. Many wine lovers prefer this style with food. The crisp version of Chardonnay tends to characterize cooler climates, and many admirers of Finger Lakes Chardonnay think its best expression is in this second group.

You can nevertheless find both styles of Chardonnay in the Finger Lakes. King Ferry Winery's Silver Lining Chardonnay is a good representative of the crisper variety, completely un-oaked (hence the "silver lining," meaning it is fermented exclusively in stainless-steel tanks), making for a pleasant, dependable wine. Other notable producers include Ravines, Heron Hill, Dr. Frank, and Anthony Road, among many others.

The popularity of Chardonnay in the wine-drinking world compels our wineries to make it central to their offerings and to work on mastering Chardonnay, a grape that is delicious and multifaceted in its best expressions, but often taken for granted.

GEWÜRZTRAMINER

Gewürztraminer—or shorthanded simply "Gewurz"—is another popular white wine in the Finger Lakes, like Riesling a wine that can go either dry or sweet. It typically exhibits a full, round, lychee-nut quality that allows it to pair well with Asian or other spicy cuisines. Gewurz is a bit of a Goldilocks grape, needing a climate neither too cold nor too hot, and can present a challenge for the grape grower hoping for a successful harvest. In the Finger Lakes we have a little over a hundred acres in cultivation, similar to Vignoles and Vidal Blanc.

GRÜNER VELTLINER

Grüner Veltliner is one of the most common grapes in Austria and, as such, would seem a natural for the similarly cool-climate region of the Finger Lakes. Yet it is a relative newcomer to the region. Only about eighteen acres in cultivation means the wine lover will have to look around for a Finger Lakes example today, although each year more Grüner is appearing on the tasting menu of Finger Lakes wineries. Grüner Veltliner is a white wine typically more rough-hewn than Riesling, but with plenty of facets that make it a good pick with a variety of foods. It also has a distinct spicy-peppery quality that blends with the fruit in a very appealing way. While not a common wine, as already noted, it is well worth seeking out: Lamoreaux Landing makes a nice Grüner Veltliner, as do Dr. Frank and Zugibe Vineyards.

LEMBERGER (aka BLAUFRÄNKISCH)

This is a red-wine grape most often found in Finger Lakes blended red wines (Shalestone's Lemberghini features this grape, along with Merlot and Syrah). Known in Europe as Blaufränkisch, where it is grown in Austria and Central European countries, Lemberger tends toward early budding, making it a tricky but not impossible grape for Finger Lakes wineries. It creates a tannic, fairly spicy wine that can be very appealing, especially paired with food. It's a relatively uncommon red grape in the area, with about thirty acres in cultivation, but many area wineries offer a Lemberger either as a varietal or in a blend. (As many tasting-room pourers will tell you, Lemberger has no relationship to Limburger cheese.)

MERLOT

Merlot is a common red-wine grape and one that appears frequently as a varietal, although it is perhaps best appreciated as part of the blend of grapes making Bordeaux. Nonetheless Merlot is a popular wine, and Finger Lakes wineries do offer it. The region has about 65 acres in cultivation (the most prevalent vinifera red being Cabernet Franc at some 220 acres), so it is far from the most common red wine here. It often appears in Finger Lakes blends. Lamoreaux Landing has a well-regarded Merlot, as do others.

MUSCAT

Another widely planted vinifera variety common in Europe but less so in the United States, Muscat divides into an array of subvarieties whose white wines tend toward sweetness. Typically Muscat is a flowery, pleasantly grapy wine that is pleasing but not complicated. It is a favorite in northern Italy, where it is used to make Asti sparkling wine, as well as in the Alsace region of France and in Austria. The most common Muscat in the Finger Lakes is a hybrid variety developed by Cornell plant scientist Bruce Reisch and released in 2006, known as Valvin Muscat, a cross between the European vinifera grape Muscat Ottonel and the hybrid Muscat du Moulin. Notable Finger Lakes producers include Hunt Country Vineyards and Ravines, but this is not a wine to be found everywhere, with only a bit over thirteen acres in cultivation. Lamoreaux Landing grows its own Muscat Ottonel. Villa Bellangelo produces the Cornell hybrid Valvin Muscat as a *frizzante* (semi-sparkling) wine.

PINOT GRIS

This is another of the Pinot family of grapes, which includes the red-wine grape Pinot Noir, but this one yields an excellent white wine that is found often in the Finger Lakes. More commonly known as Pinot Grigio in Italy, it typically yields a dry, fruity, popular wine. It's happiest in cold climates, so it is a good candidate for the Finger Lakes. The region has just over fifty acres in cultivation, making it a little less common than Merlot. Dr. Frank offers an outstanding Pinot Gris that has gathered numerous gold medals over the years. Other notable producers include Shaw, Long Point, and Thirsty Owl.

PINOT NOIR

Another of the classic vinifera grape varieties, Pinot Noir makes up the bulk of the grapes used in the great red wines of Burgundy, such as Romanée-Conti, Gevrey-Chambertin, and many others, often retailing at eye-popping prices. Fortunately you can enjoy a bottle of Finger Lakes Pinot without taking out a second mortgage on your home. Pinot Noir can be extremely tricky to grow, especially in colder climates, so it is not a go-to grape in the Finger Lakes, requiring very careful attention in the vineyard as well as the winery. But it is generally smooth and flavorful and in the right hands, and under the right conditions, becomes a complex wine at the top of any red-wine lover's wish list.

And, according to the New York Wine and Grape Foundation, "New York and especially Finger Lakes Pinot Noirs have higher levels of resveratrol (which fights heart disease and cancer) than those from other parts of the world." One of many reasons to enjoy this wine.

Most of the larger Finger Lakes wineries will have a Pinot Noir to offer. Heart & Hands, which specializes in Pinot Noir, offers outstanding examples.

RIESLING

To the average wine drinker, Riesling is far from an everyday wine. It is best known among German wines and those from the French region of Alsace, and in both locales it yields delicious wines, but German or Alsatian wines don't often show up on the table or in the cellar of the typical wine lover, at least not in comparison with other whites like Chardonnay or Sauvignon Blanc. It's a fine wine, but for most a relative afterthought.

In the Finger Lakes, however, Riesling is king.

Riesling thrives in the cool weather and stony soil of the Finger Lakes, a fact not lost on early wine producers such as Konstantin Frank and Hermann Wiemer, both of whom recognized early on that the area would be excellent for this grape. It's perhaps most interesting for the range of wines that can be produced from it. High in both sugar and acidity, Riesling can yield a rich, sweet, fruity wine or an icy-dry, complex wine with razor-sharp flavors. As a result the consumer needs to scrutinize the label carefully. Most Finger Lakes Rieslings will tell you they are dry Riesling, or semi-dry Riesling (neither sweet nor dry, a wine often at its best as an aperitif or with spicy food), or simply Riesling, which is more typically on the sweeter side but can be anywhere on the spectrum. Check the back of the bottle and one will often see a listing for "residual sugar," which is under 1 percent for dry wines and can be 5 percent or more in dessert wines. Or more conveniently, many Rieslings have a sweetness scale printed on the back, indicating where in the sweet-to-dry spectrum this particular wine falls. In whatever style, the Finger Lakes Rieslings are simply superb, and have been acknowledged so by expert wine judges worldwide. The respect that Finger Lakes wines now enjoy throughout an often hard-to-impress wine world has been forged by our Rieslings.

Riesling is the most-planted vinifera grape in the Finger Lakes, with over eight hundred acres in cultivation. Virtually every winery producing white wine in the region will offer Riesling as well, with outstanding examples coming from the fathers of Finger Lakes Rieslings, Dr. Konstantin Frank and Hermann J. Wiemer. But try any and all, and you will rarely be disappointed.

True connoisseurs enjoy aged Rieslings, which are more common among German wines but can occasionally be found in the Finger Lakes from producers who have been making wine for a long time. If you get the chance to try one, go for it. Aged Riesling—shoot for twenty years or more if you can, but close to ten will do—is a rare treat, with a distinctive petroleum element that is far more pleasing than it sounds.

IRF— the International Riesling Foundation

You'll see on some tasting menus a reference to an IRF rating. This is a designation of sweetness level given to Rieslings and promoted by the International Riesling Foundation, an industry organization dedicated to fostering appreciation of the varietal. Known as the Riesling Taste Profile, it is found on the back label of many Rieslings, a bar chart with designations of Dry, Medium Dry, Medium Sweet, and Sweet, with an arrow placed somewhere along the continuum. The winery decides where the arrow should fall, based on tastings and technical specifications such as residual sugar. The Taste Profile can be extremely helpful, since as we have seen Riesling, perhaps more than any other grape, is produced in a wide range of styles from very dry to very sweet. Wineries will typically, but not always, help out by calling a wine dry Riesling or semi-dry Riesling, but the IRF rating is considerably more exact.

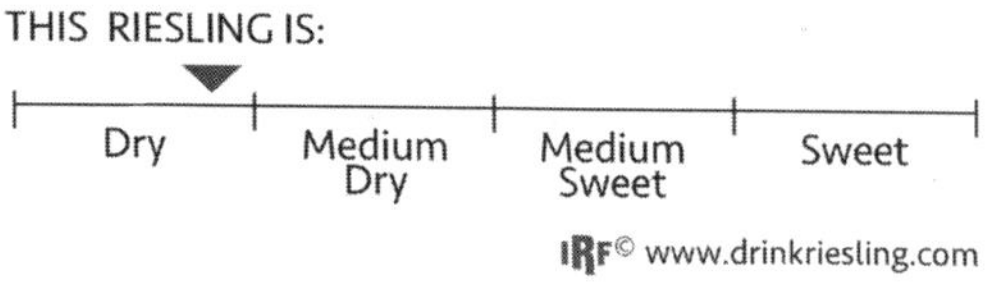

The "sweetness scale" from the International Riesling Foundation.

RKATSITELI

Just trying to pronounce this one will make you think you've perhaps had too much wine already. *Arr-katz-e-TELL-y* will come close enough for most of us for this fairly rare, ancient wine grape from the former Soviet state of Georgia. There, and throughout the wine-growing regions of Russia, it is one of the premier white-wine grapes, producing an acidic, fruity, spicy wine. Known for its cold-hardiness, Rkatsiteli has been championed here by Dr. Konstantin Frank Vinifera Wine Cellars, which grows most of the roughly ten acres of Rkatsiteli in the Finger Lakes. The winery has been producing the grape since the 1950s, and although the wines have been well received, few other Finger Lakes wineries have picked up the challenge of producing this interesting varietal. With a flavor somewhat like Gewurz, it's well worth a try.

SAPERAVI

This is a very rare wine anywhere, including the Finger Lakes, but its popularity is increasing among knowledgeable area winemakers and their fans, and deserves recognition. Saperavi hails from Ukraine and nearby regions, so it can tolerate cold, and it makes a rich, plummy red wine that can age for an extraordinary number of years. It's no surprise that a major proponent of Saperavi is Dr. Frank's, since Konstantin Frank himself came from Ukraine. Other excellent Saperavis are offered by Standing Stone and McGregor.

SAUVIGNON BLANC

While a very common grape in the overall wine world, Sauvignon Blanc is a relative rarity in the Finger Lakes, with only about seventeen acres under cultivation. Sauvignon Blanc is a popular, fruit-filled, well-balanced white wine that makes up the principal grape in French white Bordeaux. In France it is also produced under the name Pouilly-Fumé. As a varietal it is found in abundance in California, New Zealand, Chile, and many other wine-producing locations. Like Riesling, Sauvignon Blanc can be vinified in varied styles, from the very dry, grassy wines of New Zealand to the fruit-forward, almost flowery California styles. As a dessert wine Sauvignon Blanc is used (along with other grapes) to produce that ne plus ultra of dessert wines, France's Château d'Yquem.

Many of the principal vineyards in the Finger Lakes offer a Sauvignon Blanc, notably Dr. Frank, Shaw, Ravines, and others.

SYRAH (SHIRAZ)

Although Syrah is a well-known and popular red-wine vinifera grape worldwide—it makes the French Rhône wine Hermitage and the Australian Shiraz (the same grape)—it is fairly rare in the Finger Lakes. Its rarity probably owes partly to a preference for a warmer climate; anyone from southeast France or Australia will find Finger Lakes winters a bit too harsh, Syrah included. Grape growers can overcome this tendency in the case of Syrah, but it isn't easy, and often Finger Lakes Syrah tends to be picked unripe. This is unfortunate as Syrah makes a complex, tannic, full red wine that wine lovers cherish. A few Finger Lakes wineries give it a try and enjoy real success with the effort, including Atwater, Lucas, Damiani, and Hector Wine Company, on the ten acres or so of Syrah grown in the region.

Hybrid Grapes

AURORE

Yet another of Albert Seibel's approximately five hundred successful hybrids, Aurore is a white-wine grape that is the fifth most common grape grown in the Finger Lakes. It is cold-tolerant and an early ripener. Why then have few wine lovers in the area heard of it? Perhaps this is because, although at its best it can make a light, floral wine, it retains the labrusca foxiness that can make it unappealing for true table wine all by itself. It is most common in the Finger Lakes in white-wine blends, although Bully Hill and some others produce it as a varietal. Supposedly declining in cultivation in favor of other hybrids and vinifera, Aurore still boasts 545 acres.

BACO NOIR

This is a red-wine hybrid grape quite popular in the Finger Lakes. Originally created by French hybridizer François Baco in the late nineteenth or early twentieth century, Baco Noir is a deep-colored and deeply flavored red wine with a big punch, yet is relatively low in alcohol. Its fairly high acid levels make it a good candidate for cellar aging, which helps to soften the harsher edges of the wine. Baco Noir is unusual in that it is a hybrid of a white vinifera variety, Folle Blanche, and an unknown North American variety of the *Vitis riparia* species. So this French-developed grape has at least one North American parent. Baco Noir is popular in many cool-climate winemaking areas in the United States, especially Oregon, which is known for excellent examples. The Finger Lakes holds its own with Baco Noir varietals: Leidenfrost makes an excellent Baco Noir, and you can find the wine with at least several other Finger Lakes wineries. Baco Noir ranks tenth in Finger Lakes acreage, at nearly 190 acres, putting it just ahead of Pinot Noir (no relation) in red-wine grapes.

CAYUGA WHITE

Cayuga White makes a pleasant, low-alcohol wine and one very popular in the Finger Lakes region and beyond. Another of the "miracle grapes" developed by Cornell's Agricultural Experiment Station in Geneva, New York, Cayuga White is a cross between Schuyler (a labrusca variety) and the French-American hybrid Seyval Blanc. Depending upon when the grape is picked, it yields either a grapy, rather sweet white wine or something with more zest and balance, more in the Riesling family. It is used in both guises for a lot of Finger Lakes wine—it ranks just below Chardonnay in acreage, making it one of the most common sources of white table wine in the region. Cayuga White is an abundant grower and thus a favorite of grape producers. It is also a favorite of home winemakers because of its versatility and relatively easy winemaking properties. Finger Lakes winemakers use it as a varietal, generally making less expensive "sipping" wines, and in blends with Chardonnay and others to make both sparkling and still whites. Glenora takes the prize for the first commercial Cayuga White varietal, with a 1977 vintage, and they continue to produce the varietal today, as do other Finger Lakes wineries.

DE CHAUNAC

Another hybrid from the prolific Albert Seibel, this is a red-wine grape named for Canadian wine pioneer Adhémar de Chaunac, who did for Canada with hybrids what Konstantin Frank did for the Finger Lakes with vinifera. De Chaunac rarely makes a premier table wine as a varietal, although a few Finger Lakes wineries give it a try—the most notable, and successful, being J. R. Dill on Seneca Lake. For the most part it is used in blends of bulk wines, where it tends to reduce tannin levels. Perhaps for this reason there are about seventy-four acres cultivated, putting it just behind Cabernet Sauvignon in Finger Lakes acreage.

ELVIRA

In many respects Elvira is similar to Aurore, a hybrid grape that can be used to make wine and is grown plentifully in the Finger Lakes, but it is used mostly for blending and bulk wines. It's unusual in that it's an American hybrid (developed by one Jacob Rommel of Morrison, Missouri, in 1863) with elements of labrusca, riparia, and vinifera. The wine it produces is universally described as foxy, with high acid levels. Acreage is about 430, and few if any of the Finger Lakes wineries produce a varietal wine, meaning in this case a wine labeled "Elvira" and made from all, or nearly all, Elvira grapes.

MARECHAL FOCH

Another French hybrid variety, grown in the Finger Lakes primarily for its cold-hardiness, Marechal Foch (pronounced *fosh* and named in honor of the French military leader in World War I) produces a light red wine or, when more extensively vinified, a concentrated and gamy red wine. It tends to be very flowery in aroma yet much drier than one might expect on the palate. It was developed in the Alsace region of France and at one point was common in the Loire Valley, but is rarely grown there today due to European Union restrictions against using hybrid grapes in winemaking.

Finger Lakes winemakers face no such strictures and make some fine Marechal Foch varietals. Atwater produces a well-reviewed example, and you'll find Marechal Foch at Prejean, Swedish Hill, and Bully Hill. It's a relatively uncommon wine for this region (or any other region, for that matter), with about forty-seven acres in cultivation, putting it in the popularity scale of Pinot Gris or Traminette.

NOIRET

Yet another product of the Cornell Geneva Station research, Noiret is a red-wine hybrid of labrusca and vinifera, and produces a very un-hybrid, un-foxy aroma and flavor with good tannins. Noiret was released in 2006 and has about forty-two acres planted, putting it on a par with Foch, described above.

ROUGEON

Another hybrid created by the prolific nineteenth-century French hybridist Albert Seibel, Rougeon is used almost exclusively as a blending wine in the Finger Lakes. It produces a relatively dry red wine.

Vintners using Rougeon in blends include Goose Watch, Bully Hill, Prejean, Damiani, and others. It tends to mildew in the vineyard but is also an abundant producer, making it a popular grape, ranking just behind Pinot Noir at about 112 acres in cultivation.

SEYVAL BLANC

Seyval Blanc is a hybrid white-wine grape, first developed in France in the early 1920s and today grown principally in England. It is also very popular and common in the Finger Lakes, where it ranks fourth among white-wine grapes in acreage. As one might guess it is very cold-tolerant and can be harvested as early as September. Seyval Blanc makes an appealing, crisp, citrusy white wine not unlike Pinot Gris. It can be a bit thin, and winemakers sometimes try to offset this quality by aging in oak, giving the wine a bit more roundness. Many wineries in the area produce a Seyval Blanc as a varietal. Ithaca's Six Mile Creek Vineyard makes a very attractive Seyval Blanc, the perfect summer sipping wine.

Seyval Blanc has just over 180 acres in cultivation, putting it just behind Baco Noir.

TRAMINETTE

As its name implies, Traminette is related to Gewürztraminer, which is one of its "parents" along with a hybrid white called Joannes Seyve 23.416. First developed by a plant scientist the University of Illinois, H. C. Barrett, Traminette was further developed as a wine grape by Bruce Reisch and his colleagues at Cornell. It is spicy and flavorful, similar to Gewurz, but more productive, more disease-resistant, and better able to handle the Finger Lakes winters than its vinifera parent. The grape was first released in 1997.

Finger Lakes wineries have taken to Traminette in a big way, producing both blends and varietals. Hazlitt 1852 Vineyards uses it in their popular White Stag blend, and varietals come from various wineries including Fulkerson and McGregor.

Traminette is a favorite in the relatively small wine-producing region of Indiana, where it is known as "Indiana's Wine Grape." A website celebrating all-things-Traminette is to be found at www.tryontraminette.org.

VIDAL BLANC

Vidal Blanc is a hybrid variety developed to withstand harsh winters, but not specifically the winters of central New York. Vidal Blanc was developed by French hybridist Jean Louis Vidal in the 1930s, when he was looking for a grape to make cognac in western France. It is a blend of Ugni Blanc (more commonly known as Trebbiano) and a hybrid developed by the prolific Albert Seibel known as Rayon d'Or.

As the name implies, Vidal Blanc makes a white wine, generally produced as a varietal in the Finger Lakes, where it is characterized by a zesty sense of fruit and acid that is very appealing to the dry-wine drinker. Standing Stone Vineyards makes an excellent and affordable Vidal Blanc. The grape also makes an excellent ice wine, due to its cold-hardy properties, a characteristic taken up in Vidal Blanc ice wines from Knapp, Hunt Country, Wagner, and others. While not a lot of Vidal Blanc is grown in the Finger Lakes (just over a hundred acres), that still puts it among the top ten grapes used to make white wine. It is a pleasant wine, good with food, and well worth adding to the cellar.

VIGNOLES

This is an uncommon grape outside of the Finger Lakes, but a popular one here. Vignoles (pronounced *vin-YOLE*, and given its name by the Finger Lakes Wine Growers Association in 1970, before which it was known by the less-euphonious Ravat-51) is a sweet but interesting and fruity white wine that pairs really well with spicy Asian cuisine. It also makes a delicious ice wine and is often seen as a late-harvest vintage. The vine buds late in the season, making it a natural for our area. In the Finger Lakes we have just over a hundred acres of Vignoles, putting in the top twenty of our varieties.

Labrusca Grapes

Labrusca is Latin for "wild," and sure enough these are the grapes that grow naturally in the region. Finger Lakes growers produce loads of labrusca grapes, most of which go into making grape juice, jams and jellies, and in many cases wine. If you want to know what *foxy* means, try wine made from one of these—Concord, Catawba, or Niagara are the principal varieties in the region—and you'll know it instantly. To be fair, some palates like the foxy flavor, and many Finger Lakes wineries produce sweet red and white wines that will appeal to them. But the more experienced wine drinker will soon find them tiresome. A labrusca wine is inevitably grapy—that foxiness again—and has a single-faceted, monochromatic quality. It's the wine drinker's equivalent of painting every room in the house pale yellow. Despite these qualities Concord takes the prize as the most-planted grape in the region, with over 1,800 acres, with Catawba at 800 or so, and Niagara around 650. From the vinifera team, only Riesling, at about 825 acres, can compete with the labruscas.

Lamoreaux Landing Wine Cellars, Seneca Lake

Glenora Wine Cellars, Seneca Lake. The first Seneca Lake winery.

Barrel room, Dr. Konstantin Frank Vinifera Wine Cellars

Grape blossoms, the beginning of grape clusters.

Developing grapes, July (Riesling)

Ready for harvest (Chardonnay)

Crusher and barrel room, Wagner Vineyards, Seneca Lake

The pot still at Knapp Winery, Cayuga Lake

Thirsty Owl Wine Company, Cayuga Lake

Standing Stone Vineyards, Seneca Lake

Tank room, Ryan William Vineyard, Seneca Lake

Heron Hill Winery, Keuka Lake

McGregor Vineyard, Keuka Lake

Vines "hilled up" for winter protection.
Hermann J. Wiemer Vineyard, Seneca Lake

Red Tail Ridge Winery, Seneca Lake

Tierce, a collaboration among Anthony Road, Fox Run, and Red Newt.

The deck view from Lamoreaux Landing Wine Cellars, Seneca Lake

King Ferry Winery, Cayuga Lake

The heart of the Banana Belt, Chateau LaFayette Reneau, Seneca Lake

Ithaca's Ports of New York

Winter vines, Ontario County

Harvest time, Silver Thread Vineyard, Seneca Lake

Shaw Vineyard, Seneca Lake

2 | *A (Very) Short Course in Making Wine*

MAKING BAD WINE is simple: Crush grapes, allow the juice to sit around for a while, strain it and bottle it, and you're all set. Making good wine is considerably more complicated, and while this book cannot get into all the details of winemaking, it is valuable to examine the most common winemaking practices one might encounter while learning about and drinking Finger Lakes wines.

Let's begin in the vineyard. A year or two after grapevines are planted, grapes will appear. The vines need sun (but not too much or too little), rain (but not too much or too little), some good luck, and loads of careful attention from the people in charge of the vineyard. (Granted, growing grapes is every bit as complicated as making wine, perhaps more so, but let's stick to winemaking.) As September arrives the winemaker begins sampling the grapes, looking for the balance of sweetness and acidity that will be right for the wine in question. At last the grapes are perfect and it's time to pick. Here comes a choice: pick by hand or pick by machine?

The answer will be dictated by economics, the size of the vineyard, the availability of harvest workers, and many other things. Most grapes are harvested by machines and make perfectly good wine. Some grapes, such as Pinot Noir, are more tender than others and may have to be handpicked. The very best wine grapes will probably be harvested

Chardonnay collected in bins and then tipped into the crusher-destemmer.

by hand, but machine-harvesting is no reason to avoid a wine or a winery.

The harvested grapes are collected into bins and brought to the winery. There the grapes are dumped into a crusher-destemmer, which does just what it says: crushes the grapes and takes them off the stems.

Up to this point the process has been the same whether the winery is making white wine or red. But after this point, the techniques will be very different. Let's start with white wines, or at least most white wines (as we said, making good wine is complicated).

For a white wine such as Riesling the crusher-destemmer does its work and the result goes into the wine press. Most modern wine presses extract the grape juice very gently, and the juice can be separated by when it emerges: the first juice, called free-run, is the most acidic and generally the best. The juice that comes afterward is progressively less acidic, and some winemakers will separate the free-run juice from the rest.

The next step is a settling tank, which allows the bits of stem, skins, and seeds to settle to the bottom. Once that happens the grape juice is pumped into a stainless-steel tank. These tanks can be small or large, but often they are about two to five thousand gallons in capacity. The tanks do not need to be, and generally are not, totally full. But they must be kept at the correct temperature in order for the next step, fermentation, to happen in the right way.

Now the winemaker has a choice. The grape juice needs yeast in order for fermentation to begin. Until the 1960s, just about all wine was made using what is called wild, native, or indigenous yeast—this was yeast that occurred naturally in the environment and was already on the grapes at harvest. Some winemakers today, especially those who subscribe to the minimal-intervention school of winemaking, will wait for the indigenous yeasts to do their work in almost all circumstances. But this approach has its drawbacks: The yeast can take a long time to get started, and in the meantime the wine can spoil. Or the native yeast may not act the way the winemaker wants. The alternative, which is practiced by the great majority of winemakers today throughout the world—including the Finger Lakes—is to "inoculate," as it's called, the juice with commercially prepared yeast that will start fermentation right away and can be counted on to perform in predictable ways.

The wait begins. The wine will ferment and is monitored frequently. Temperature control is critical. In fermentation, the sugars inherent in the grape juice are turned to alcohol. The winemaker is waiting for the balance of sugar, alcohol level, and other wine-flavor components to unite in the best possible way. It is in making this call, when to stop fermentation, that winemakers earn their spurs.

One other option is to allow a secondary fermentation, called malolactic fermentation (frequently abbreviated simply as MLF), to occur. Malolactic fermentation converts malic acid (tasting like a crisp green apple) to lactic acid (the acid in yogurt), resulting in a rounder, creamier sort of mouthfeel. Chardonnay lends itself well to this secondary fermentation.

Once fermentation is complete the wine needs to age, allowing the various flavor components to come together, just as a soup or stew will taste better if refrigerated overnight and reheated the next day. Wines need time to settle down. Some white wines will age in stainless-steel tanks, some in oak barrels, some in a combination of the two. This choice is again up to the winemaker and can be a delicate one.

Back to red wines. The major difference between red and white wine is not only the grape variety but how long the pressed juice is left in contact with the grape skins. White wines are made with the skins removed right after crushing, but reds are left in contact with the skins, and sometimes the stems as well, for a period of time—how much time is again the call of the winemaker. It is this skin contact that gives the wine its color.

The red wine is then fermented much like the white, except at somewhat higher temperatures. Reds can be fermented in tanks or often in oak barrels, and typically for reds a malolactic, secondary fermentation occurs. When fermentation is complete the wine is usually transferred to an oak barrel to age. Reds typically age longer than whites, sometimes for a couple of years or more. Again this is up to the winemaker, and candidly often up to the business needs of the winery. If they need bottles on the shelves, there will be pressure to get the wine bottled and sold sooner rather than later.

Barrels are (believe it or not) a complicated subject. There are differences in the quality and flavor characteristics of wines aged in barrels from different places—common barrel sources are France, America, and Hungary. Oak barrels are typically charred on the inside to enhance their flavor character, and this charring (known as the toast) can be light, medium, or heavy. A fresh barrel that has never had wine in it will impart a lot of oak flavor, while one that has been used many times will impart very little or none. The latter barrel is what is referred to as a neutral barrel. Whether wine lovers need to know, or care, about the details of barrel aging is up to them, but any wine drinker will care about the level of oak because that affects the flavor of the wine. Many wines today are over-oaked, which tends to mask flavor flaws in the wine. Fortunately this is not a common occurrence in

the Finger Lakes, but it does happen in wines from other areas. Oak should be a flavor enhancer, not the main taste of the wine.

After aging the wine is typically fined, which involves adding an organic, inert component to remove impurities, and then filtered (some natural-wine proponents try to avoid filtering) to remove any odd bits. Sulfur dioxide is also added to the wine to prevent spoilage in case bacteria of any kind is present. Keeping the sulfur to a minimum is generally the goal of good winemakers. There is a belief that too much sulfur dioxide promotes hangovers, although the evidence for this being true is not fully clear.

Then it is on to bottling. Many Finger Lakes wineries have their own bottling line, but the equipment is expensive and must be kept scrupulously hygienic. Many smaller wineries contract out the bottling to another, larger winery, or even use a "mobile bottling" facility that resides inside a large truck that pulls up to the winery and takes care of the chore right there.

The subject of closures—whether to use natural cork, or some cork amalgam, or plastic, or screw-tops—is too detailed a subject for this book. But it is worth noting that many wines, especially Rieslings and other whites, are bottled using a screw-cap closure. Don't be put off by this: Twenty years ago the screw-cap was a tip-off to cheap wine, but that's not the case today. Many quality wines are bottled with screw-caps, all around the world, including the Finger Lakes. Good screw-caps will last many years—ten or more—and keep the wine just as snug as a natural cork.

Sparkling Wine and Méthode Champenoise

There are various ways to make a wine sparkling, the easiest and most economical being to inject it with carbon dioxide (carbonation), which produces a carbonated beverage, in this case wine, like those we're all familiar with. There are some carbonated Rieslings and white blends made by a few Finger Lakes wineries, and they make for a pleasant enough change of pace.

Other ways of making sparkling wine are more complicated and time consuming, sometimes much more so. The critical step to any sparkling wine of this type is a secondary fermentation in a tightly closed container that produces a natural effervescence. One means of doing this, which is used for Prosecco, is called the Charmat or (in Italy) the Martinotti method. Here the secondary fermentation takes place in a stainless-steel tank and the wine is bottled under pressure. The third way to make sparkling wine, which is most often employed in the Finger Lakes, is the most time consuming and expensive but, generally speaking, produces the best wine. This method is known as *méthode champenoise*.

Méthode champenoise is of course French for "champagne method" and it may be seen on the labels of many Finger Lakes sparkling wines. Here white wine is fermented in tanks, then transferred to a heavy, thick-sided bottle. Yeast and sugar are added to prompt a secondary fermentation, and the bottle is capped. The bottles are stored horizontally for a long time—years in some cases, especially at top champagne houses in France.

Once the wine has undergone its secondary fermentation and aging, the next step involves getting the yeast particles out. The bottles are put into a rack, neck-first and at a slight downward angle. Each day or two, every bottle is twisted just a bit to keep the lees (the leftover yeast particles) from sticking to the sides. (This process, known as riddling, is done by hand if quantities are low, but is often mechanized—it makes little to no difference.) As the bottles are twisted, they are also gradually pointed downward, until they are completely upside down. There they sit, sometimes for as long as years in the top champagne houses, until the yeast has collected into a dense mass at the cap. The necks of the bottles are frozen, the cap is removed and the yeast plug pulled out, the bottle is topped up, and a champagne cork and wire enclosure is applied to keep the effervescent wine where it belongs until opening.

And you wondered why sparkling wines are expensive?

3 | *Month-by-Month in a Finger Lakes Winery*

THERE IS A LOT MORE that goes on in a winery than is listed here, but this monthly checklist will give some idea of the range of issues facing the typical Finger Lakes winery. We could add, in every month, the job of marketing the wines, which might involve Wine Trail events, website updating, case-club member promotions, and anything else the winery owners and their team can do to help spread the word about their wines and the Finger Lakes wine scene in general.

JANUARY	Keep an eye on the fermentation tanks and barrels. The vines are dormant. By now, in most years, snow covers the vineyard.
FEBRUARY	In the winery, some of the wines are still fermenting. In the vineyard, prune the vines, if the weather cooperates.
MARCH	Keep pruning the vines. Hope for a mild winter. Tank and barrel samples are taken to judge the progress of the wines.
APRIL	Bottling begins on fully finished wines from last year's harvest, especially the whites. Finish pruning the vines.
MAY	Sometime in mid-May, bud break. The vines come alive. The frost-watch begins: If frost hits hard after bud break, the yield will be reduced, sometimes by large amounts. The cold temperatures in the lakes help delay bud break until May takes hold and the danger of frost is past. This date varies by region and

	even from vineyard to vineyard, but by May 15, in most cases, the danger of frost is over. In the winery, more bottling, which will continue through the summer.
JUNE	Grapes appear, first in little clusters, growing larger as the days pass.
JULY	Watch out for mildew in the vineyard if the weather is wet. Hope for rain if the weather is dry. Grapes are beginning to ripen. Canopy management—removing leaves to maximize sun exposure—kicks into gear.
AUGUST	More canopy management, more ripening, more concern about mildew and dryness.
SEPTEMBER	The harvest-watch begins, and with it the busiest time of year for a winery. How ripe are the grapes? Do they need more time? What if it rains buckets, which will dilute the flavor in the grapes and make the vintage uninspiring? At some point, the winery will commit to a time to harvest and get started. At this point, it's all hands on deck. Grapes need to be picked, then crushed. Tanks are filled; winemakers are busy eighteen hours per day.
OCTOBER	For some vineyards, more harvest, more crushing. Tanks are monitored. The tasting room is at its busiest, with an influx of "leaf-peeper" visitors up for a weekend in the Finger Lakes. Sometime before it snows, the vines need to be hilled up—covered over with earth above the graft to protect against the coming winter.
NOVEMBER	Late-harvest grapes are harvested.
DECEMBER	As always, monitor the tanks and barrels. Barrel-aged reds and whites are transferred from stainless-steel tanks to oak barrels. They can remain in barrels for months or years, depending on the wine and the goals of the winemaker. Clean and maintain vineyard equipment and settle back for the holidays.

4 | *Specialty Wines and Sidelines*

MOST WINES made at Finger Lakes wineries are table wines like Chardonnay or Cabernet Franc, the varieties we normally think of when we think about wine. But the world of wine is much broader than table wines alone, and includes dessert wines, fruit wines, mead (wine made from honey), fortified wines, and more. While this book covers these wines only in passing, it's worth examining a few of these non-table-wine products, which are emblematic of the diversity and dynamic spirit of the Finger Lakes wineries.

Dessert Wines

Many Finger Lakes wineries produce a dessert wine of some kind. One way to spot a dessert wine is to look at the amount of residual sugar, abbreviated RS, in the wine. Residual sugar somewhere around 4 percent or more is sweetness typical of a dessert wine. The RS percentage can be very high with an intensely sweet wine—20 percent RS and more. Often, though not always, dessert wines are produced from Riesling, Vignoles, or other white-wine grapes. Almost always, these dessert wines are bottled in 375ml bottles, and are considerably more expensive than the average bottle of table wine.

Commonly you'll see dessert wine in one of three categories: late-harvest wine, ice wine, and iced wine. The distinctions are important. A late-harvest wine is just that: a wine whose grapes are harvested late, after the grapes have begun to shrivel and the sugars to concentrate. Late-harvest grapes are picked by hand and picked carefully to sort out good grapes from bad. A late-harvest wine might come in at 4 or 5 percent RS.

Ice wine takes the late-harvest concept and goes it one better. Rather than picking when the grapes are shriveled, the maker of ice wine waits until the grapes are literally frozen. Not any frozen grape will do, of course, and some grapes simply rot before they freeze. Even rot, of a kind, can be helpful, as with the famous "noble rot," Botrytis cinerea, which is a fungus that can appear on grapes late in the season and helps concentrate the sugars and flavors in ice wine. Needless to say, Nature doesn't always cooperate in making ice wine, but when it does, the results can be spectacular. RS levels in ice wine can be 20 percent or more. Due to the meticulous care involved in making it, and the scarcity of available grapes, ice wine can be quite expensive.

Iced wine, by contrast, is made from a sweeter grape, perhaps a late-harvest grape, but the wine is frozen so the winemaker can lift out the water that has turned to ice, concentrating the flavor and sweetness of the wine in the process. There is nothing artificial about iced wine, but it will never have the complexity or elegance of a well-made ice wine. The winery will be forthright about the difference, and will list a wine as an iced wine if in fact that's what it is. As you'd expect, iced wines are less expensive than ice wines.

Sparkling Wines

Many Finger Lakes wineries produce sparkling wines, which are discussed in the profiles of the wineries that follow. As we have seen (page

69), producing sparkling wine can be a complex process, and as a result most sparkling wines are more expensive than still (non-sparkling) wines. Generally sparklers are made from a blend of white wines, usually including Chardonnay. An all-Chardonnay sparkling wine is known as a blanc de blancs. A sparkling white wine made from Pinot Noir is called a blanc de noirs.

Rosé, Blush, and Orange Wines

These are three seemingly similar wines made in three distinctly different ways.

Rosé is made from red-wine grapes vinified in a white-wine style. Pinot Noir is a common rosé grape. The juice is left on the skins for a relatively short period of time, perhaps a day or two, then taken off the skins and moved to a tank for fermentation. Many Finger Lakes wineries are producing rosé wines, which are increasingly popular.

Orange wine is made from white-wine grapes vinified in a red-wine style. Again the major difference is time on the skins. Orange wines are left in contact with the skins for an extended period of time. Typically for white wine the juice is drained off the skins right away. Orange wine—sometimes known as ambered—is pretty rare in the Finger Lakes (and anywhere else).

Blush wine is a combination of white wine and red wine. Although in appearance a blush wine is very similar to a rosé, the process is very different. You can make a "blush" wine in your own wineglass by adding a little red to a greater amount of white. Makers of blush wines take more care than that, and the results can be perfectly pleasant sipping wines, but a blush wine will never have the taste, complexity, and interest of a well-made rosé. (In France, where as we know they take wine very seriously, it is against the law to produce blush wine. France does produce much of the world's best rosé.)

Fruit Wines and Mead

These wines are outside of the scope of this book, but visitors to Finger Lakes wineries will often see wines made from apples, blueberries, or other fruit. Sheldrake, for example, offers a very nice apple dessert wine, and Hosmer has a terrific dessert wine made from raspberries. Mead, a wine made from honey, is pretty scarce but does appear here. Lakewood produces a very interesting mead.

Port and Sherry

A substantial number of Finger Lakes wineries produce port, or a variety of it, which consists mostly of adding distilled spirits to a partially fermented wine. The spirits themselves come from distilling wine in a pot-still, a large, orb-shaped metal vessel set over a gas fire, which boils the wine very slowly and drips out the distilled spirit. Traditional (Portuguese) high-quality port is made with extreme care, often using age-old methods, and is typically aged for years. Finger Lakes port producers are not making wines at this level of complexity. Most ports in the Finger Lakes are interesting and enjoyable dessert wines, but they are not in the same league as true port. One exception is Ithaca's Ports of New York, discussed below, which makes port exclusively and has significantly raised the bar for port in the region.

Less common in the Finger Lakes is sherry, and again what is made here is not truly in the same category as genuine sherry from Spain. Sherry is made in what is called the solera method, where wine is put into barrels after fermentation for aging. The solera system involves combining old and new wine. The fermented wine is kept in barrels stacked in a triangle shape. The "solera" itself consists of the row of oak barrels on the bottom, containing the oldest wine, with progressively younger wines stacked in rows above, the youngest on top. Wine from the bottom (oldest) row is taken out for bottling, but the barrels are only partially emptied. These are then filled up with wine from the barrels in the row above, which in turn is filled from the row above it, and so on. So the wines never stand on their own but are "built up" by the older wines below them. It is a complicated and interesting process, more involved than we have explained here. While Finger Lakes sherry can't compete with the wines of Spain, many of the examples made here are rich and interesting. One surprising source of excellent solera-made sherry is the Hazlitt Red Cat Winery in Naples, discussed below, which has a solera on the roof of the winery.

Cider, Beer, and Spirits

While these beverages fall outside the scope of this book, anyone driving through Finger Lakes wine country will find cideries, breweries, and spirits-makers in abundance along the route. One cidery not to be missed is Bellwether, which is discussed below in connection with their recently introduced wines. Apples are a major crop in this part of New York State, so the cider industry finds a natural home here. Some years ago hops were also a significant crop here, and there are now a few breweries bringing back hops to the region, as well as many others making a full menu of craft beers. Distilled spirits, often distilling grape wines from the region, are also a burgeoning business. One of the first, and best, is Finger Lakes Distilling on Seneca Lake, right in the heart of Seneca's wine country. Finger Lakes Distilling makes vodka, gin, whiskey, and other spirits, all from local grapes, fruits, and grains.

PART III
Wineries of the Finger Lakes

IT IS DIFFICULT to keep count of the number of wineries in the Finger Lakes, because a new one seems to open every couple of weeks. The wineries profiled in this book are a subjective list of those that the reasonably serious wine enthusiast will want to learn about and explore. Virtually all of them are small, family-run businesses, very often a husband-and-wife team either native to the region or people who fell in love with the Finger Lakes, as so many do, and wanted to own a vineyard or winery here. Some wineries have been active for thirty years or more; others are nearly brand new. But what characterizes these enterprises without exception is a commitment to the region and its wines, to making them a bit better each vintage year, all the while reaching out to the rest of the wine world and increasingly getting its attention.

The wineries are organized by lake, and we deal here only with Cayuga, Seneca, and Keuka Lakes. The other Finger Lakes have wineries here and there, but the main focus of attention is on the wineries clustered around these three. The reasons for this concentration involve soils, microclimates, the lake depths, and history. The best soils for growing grapes tend to be found around these three central lakes. This statement is not absolute by any means—there are many vineyards on or near Canandaigua, Skaneateles, and other lakes that produce

outstanding grapes. But as a general rule the majority of vineyards are clustered in this region. So, too, are the mysteries of weather, which for example produces the "Banana Belt" region in southeastern Seneca Lake and works its magic to soften the blows of winter in other areas as well. The "lake effect," which as we have seen is instrumental in tempering the effects of cold, is felt most profoundly on the two deepest lakes, Seneca and Cayuga. And history has destined many important wineries to be located on Keuka Lake. As we've seen, Finger Lakes wines began on Keuka Lake, first with the Reverend William P. Bostwick and later with Pleasant Valley, Gold Seal, and Taylor's, which in turn led to Bully Hill, Dr. Konstantin Frank, and many other premier wineries today.

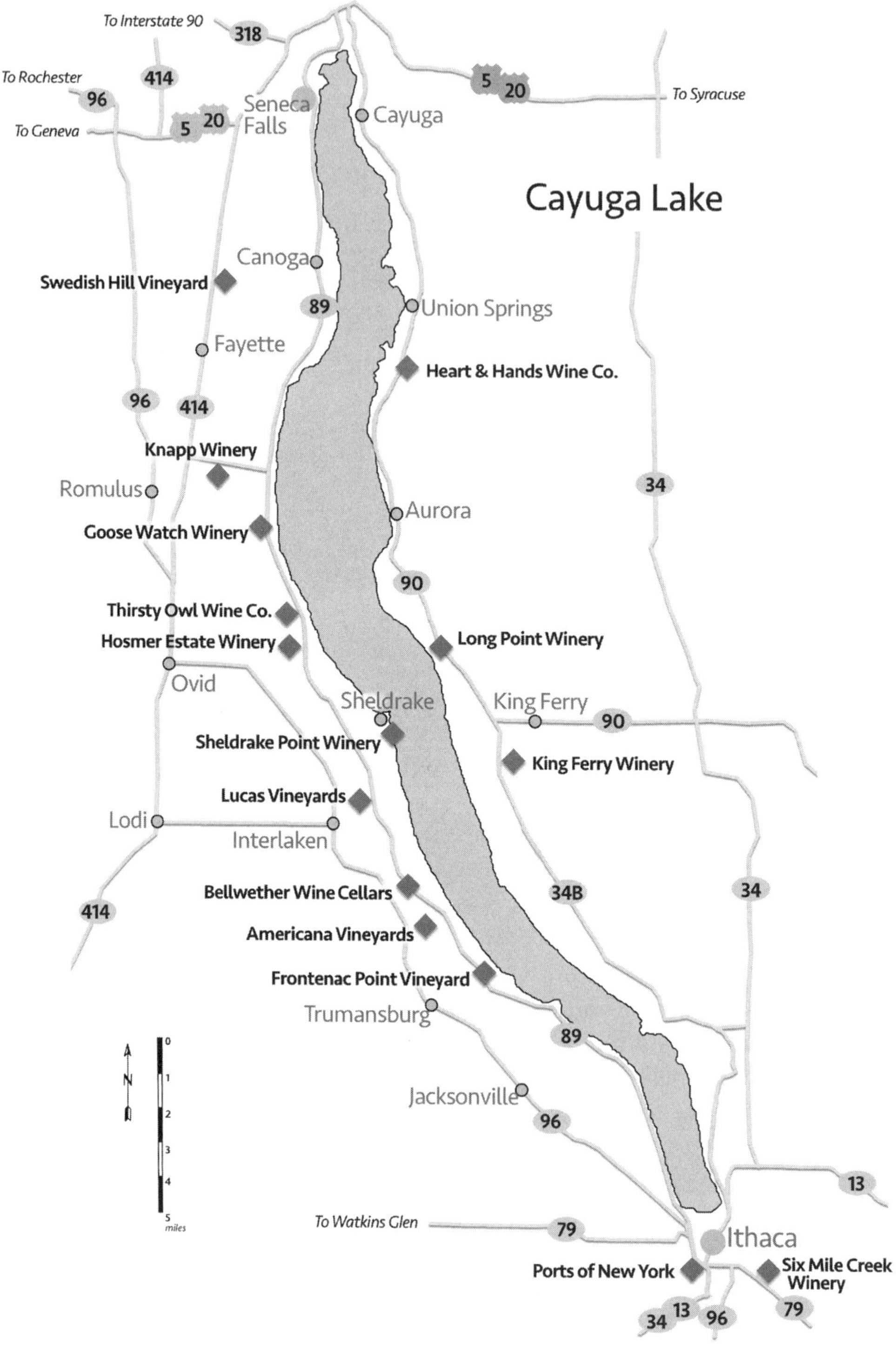
Cayuga Lake
To Interstate 90
318
414
To Rochester
96
To Geneva
5
20
Seneca Falls
Cayuga
To Syracuse
Canoga
Swedish Hill Vineyard
89
Union Springs
Fayette
Heart & Hands Wine Co.
96
414
Knapp Winery
Romulus
34
Aurora
Goose Watch Winery
90
Thirsty Owl Wine Co.
Hosmer Estate Winery
Long Point Winery
Ovid
Sheldrake
King Ferry
Sheldrake Point Winery
King Ferry Winery
Lucas Vineyards
Lodi
Interlaken
34B
34
414
Bellwether Wine Cellars
Americana Vineyards
Frontenac Point Vineyard
Trumansburg
89
Jacksonville
96
13
To Watkins Glen
79
Ithaca
Ports of New York
Six Mile Creek Winery
34
13
96
79
N
0
1
2
3
4
5
miles

1 | *Cayuga Lake Wineries*

CAYUGA LAKE is the longest of the Finger Lakes, at about thirty-eight miles, and the second deepest, at 435 feet, so the "lake effect" of relative warmth in the winter and cooling in the spring is definitely in play here. Cayuga is home to some early wineries, such as Lucas, Frontenac Point, Swedish Hill, and others, and launched the very first Wine Trail in the Finger Lakes, in 1983. Today Cayuga hosts a great variety of facilities that offer the wine lover an intriguing range of wines and winemaking styles. Bellwether, Sheldrake, Treleaven, Heart & Hands, and Hosmer are among the wineries that reward a visit here.

Americana Vineyards & Winery

Americana is the second-oldest winery on Cayuga Lake, founded by an Ithaca College professor, James Treble, in 1981 and growing native-grape varieties (therefore the name Americana); the winery was purchased by the current owner, Joe Gober, in the late 1990s. The vineyards are now gone—the vines had not been kept up, and all were native-grape varieties. Gober wanted to expand to vinifera and hybrids to match the tastes of contemporary wine drinkers. So the vineyards were removed—but they remain on the label. There you see vineyards depicted, and in the lower left corner is the roof edge of a building. This building is what's now the Crystal Lake Café, next to the tasting room.

There is in fact also no winery here: Americana wines are made at Lakewood Vineyards, on Seneca Lake, by the winemaker there, Chris Stamp, in consultation with Joe Gober.

Americana has active plans to bring back a vineyard, however, and is planting six acres in the old site behind the tasting room and restaurant. This is to ensure availability and to restore the "Vineyards" to Americana Vineyards. They are also planning to plant hops—beer became a sideline after the acquisition of Bacchus Brewing Co. of Dryden. A tasting room for the beer is now downstairs.

Americana has a pleasantly informal tasting room and an active music and social scene. Wines include a Chablis (a blend of Chardonnay and Cayuga White), a Chardonnay, Gewurz, Riesling, and Pinot Gris in the whites, and a nice Baco Noir varietal, Lemberger, Cabernet Franc, and Cabernet Sauvignon in the reds, along with a red blend of hybrids, Revolutionary Red. Various sweet and semi-sweet white and red wines are also offered, including their popular red, Sweet Rosie, made with the native Ives grape.

Americana produces something over 12,000 cases per year.

Bellwether Wine Cellars

Bellwether is a well-known name among Finger Lakes culinary devotees, for the hard cider produced there rather than for wine—but that is changing rapidly. Bellwether Hard Ciders, which began in 1999 and moved to their current location on Route 89 in Trumansburg in 2003, produces about ten different types of (mostly) carbonated hard ciders, which are unfortunately outside the scope of this book. How they got into wine is an interesting transition story, which has all to do with owners Cheryl and Bill Barton's son-in-law, winemaker Kris Mathewson.

Mathewson is a young man, but already has worked with fifteen Finger Lakes vintages. His winemaking career began with his college years at SUNY Utica, when he worked four summers at Bully Hill. This led him to pursue wine as a career, with positions at Heron Hill, Swedish Hill, and Atwater Vineyards, where he became assistant winemaker and started getting serious attention for his wines. (Blogger Maggie Davidson writes in *Serious Eats*, for example, that "On my first visit to New York's Finger Lakes several years ago, one wine stood out: a single-vineyard Riesling offered by the young assistant winemaker at Atwater Estate Vineyards [Kris Mathewson]. Nothing else compared.") Head-turning stuff, yet Mathewson is a friendly, down-to-earth sort, happy to talk wine and the joys and tribulations of making it in the Finger Lakes.

Bellwether is now officially known as Bellwether Hard Cider and Wine Cellars, and the labels on the wines say simply "Bellwether Wine Cellars." Mathewson produces Rieslings and Pinot Noir for now, in very limited quantities—generally fewer than two hundred cases per wine. As a result, he concedes, his wines can be expensive—in a rare instance at or near $100 per bottle. (Wine lovers on a more realistic budget can pick themselves off the floor—several of the Bellwether wines are available in the $19–25 range, not out of line for a finely crafted wine with limited production.) Still in the aging cellar is a new wine, a sparkling Chardonnay, aged for five years, to be released in 2017.

The tasting room at Bellwether offers a few of the wines but, again owing to limited production, there are wines available for sale that do not make it to the tasting menu. And many wines are selling out quickly or making their way to Manhattan restaurants, where high retail prices are less of a barrier. (*Bon Appétit*, for example, opined that "tiny Bellwether Wine Cellars is bottling the best German-style Riesling outside of Germany . . . It's quickly becoming a cult wine, so if you find it, stock up.") Speaking of Germany, Mathewson admits his goal for the Riesling is to see it sold and appreciated there, the "home port" of great Rieslings.

We will leave it to others to say what the "best" Riesling might be, but without question this is outstanding, carefully crafted wine. Mathewson employs wild fermentation where possible (allowing naturally occurring yeasts to launch the fermentation process), and sources his grapes from vineyards throughout the region, drawing on a pool of vineyards and growers that he knows well and has worked with for some years. Bellwether has multi-year contracts to purchase grapes from specific acreage, so Mathewson knows what he is getting and can build upon the experience of prior vintages. Also, his closeness with the growers gives him the confidence that the vineyard practices are sound.

Alex Ulreich

All wines are single-vineyard wines—Mathewson wants the vineyardists to receive credit. Among them are A&D Vineyard, on Keuka Lake; Seneca Lake's Tuller Vineyard (whose earliest vines—older than the winemaker himself—date to 1976); and Seven Sisters Vineyard.

Bellwether Wine Cellars produces about 2,000 cases a year at present, with a goal of about 3,000. But clearly quality is a far higher priority than quantity. This is still a small winery, but for the serious wine drinker interested in the upper end of Finger Lakes winemaking, the tasting room is an important and rewarding destination.

Frontenac Point Vineyard

Frontenac Point Vineyard has been around a long time, by Finger Lakes standards, starting up just a couple of years after the 1976 Farm Winery Act was passed. Owners Jim and Carol Doolittle purchased the land that was to become their vineyard on New Year's Day, 1978, and in 1982 had their first vintage. Jim Doolittle had firsthand knowledge of the act, having been instrumental in its development. In the 1970s Jim was working for the New York State Department of Agriculture and Markets and wrote a paper outlining the advantages of such a law. His paper was prompted by market troubles in the Finger Lakes grape industry: Prices for grapes had fallen from something like $275 per ton to about

$75 per ton.The paper found its way to department commissioner John Dyson, who recommended to New York governor Hugh Carey that an act would be helpful. Doolittle met with Lieutenant Governor Mary Ann Krupsak, whom Carey had asked to get the legislation started. Doolittle and Krupsak worked for eighteen months, holding meetings with wine industry figures and legislators, and eventually developed the Farm Winery Act. Much of the credit for jump-starting the Finger Lakes wine industry we know today is owed to Jim Doolittle.

Frontenac Point is strictly an estate winery, making wine exclusively from their own grapes grown in their eighteen-acre vineyard. Their focus is on dry wines, from both vinifera and hybrids, including various incarnations of Chambourcin, a rarely encountered red hybrid that Frontenac makes as a varietal, a rosé, and adds to blends. Their Proprietor's Reserve is a blend of hybrids Chambourcin, Marechal Foch, and Chelois. Frontenac Red, another blend, combines the Foch and Chambourcin with Pinot Noir. Among the whites are a Chardonnay, Riesling, Seyval Blanc, Vignoles, and a blend, Stay Sail, which combines Gewurz with a bit of Riesling. They also make a dessert port, using Chambourcin again, with distilled Seyval Blanc spirits.

Frontenac Point Vineyard produces about 2,000 to 3,000 cases of wine per year.

Goose Watch Winery

Goose Watch Winery was launched in 1997 by owners Dave and Jean Peterson, who also own Swedish Hill and Penguin Bay. Surrounded by chestnut trees, the tasting room is housed in a restored barn and features nice views of Cayuga Lake below. (There is also a dock at the waterline with easy access to the winery for the boating wine lover.) Around the winery are twenty-one acres of vineyards that produce most of the grapes for Goose Watch. This vineyard grows Viognier, Lemberger (the first Lemberger in New York State, planted in the early

1990s), Chambourcin, Melody, Pinot Noir, and Traminette. As this list might indicate, Goose Watch is home to some unusual varieties. The winery slogan is "Where tradition and innovation meet," meaning they offer traditional vinifera and native varietals but also new and unusual wines, such as Aromella and Melody, which you rarely find elsewhere.

Aromella (the name is a nod to *aroma*, which is borne out by the powerful nose on this wine) is very floral on the nose but drier than might be expected in the glass. This grape was developed by Cornell and the Geneva Experiment Station and released in 2013. Goose Watch produced the first varietal of Aromella, and the wine well rewards a try. The winery also hosted test plots of the grape as it was being developed. Melody is another Cornell product, developed in the 1980s, a white-wine grape still somewhat rare as a varietal but again well worth a try.

Also on offer at Goose Watch are a Riesling-Gewurz blend, a Viognier and a Traminette (both hybrids, the latter again from Cornell), a Pinot Grigio, and a nice Cab Franc rosé. Dry reds include a Merlot, Lemberger, Cabernet Sauvignon, and the relatively rare red hybrid Chambourcin. On the sweet side they have various sweeter native and hybrid whites; among the reds is a Red Moscato, the first in the Finger Lakes.

Dessert wines include a rare (again) white port and a cream sherry made in the solera method, using wine from older barrels to start the new. This sherry is fortified with brandy made at Swedish Hill. The cream sherry contains Catawba, some Chardonnay, Niagara, and other grapes.

Goose Watch produces about 15,000 cases of wine per year. The winemaker here (as well as at Swedish Hill and Penguin Bay) is Derek Wilber; he has held the position for some time, now joined by Zach Pegram.

Goose Watch is host to a fun and informal Classic Car Show in July, and in October they showcase the seventeen acres of nut groves on the property with a Chestnut Festival, featuring all-things-chestnut.

Heart & Hands Wine Company

Heart & Hands is a relative newcomer to the Finger Lakes wine scene, launching in 2008, but a welcome one with an interesting twist. Rather than offer a range of the wines that can be made here, owner Tom Higgins and his wife, Susan, have chosen to focus on two wines only, Riesling and Pinot Noir. Both are made with a high degree of success.

Tom Higgins is a Finger Lakes native who worked at Hazlitt 1852 Vineyards while still in high school, adding considerably to that experience with stints in Bordeaux, California, and back in the Finger Lakes at Thirsty Owl and Atwater.

The name Heart & Hands derives from the Higginses' Celtic background. The heart-and-hand symbol that appears on a traditional Irish wedding band also appears on the label of all their wines. Set on sloping terrain at the east side of Cayuga Lake, Heart & Hands has a relatively small four-acre vineyard comprising about three acres of Pinot Noir and one of Riesling. The majority of their grapes come from growers based on Seneca, Cayuga, and Skaneateles Lakes.

Their wines are very well made with meticulous attention to detail. Grapes are handpicked and sorted, gently pressed, and (for the Pinot) aged in oak for at least twelve months. The Pinots are typically unfiltered. Their first estate Pinot Noir was released in 2015 and called Mo Chuisle, Gaelic for "my pulse" or, more informally, "my darling." This wine receives particular TLC, with multiple passes made through the vineyard hand-selecting perfectly ripe grapes, whole-cluster fermentation, and (for the 2012 vintage) twenty months in oak before bottling. Any of their selections is rewarding, but don't miss the unusual white wine called Polarity. This is a Pinot Noir, a red-wine grape, vinified as a white wine.

Heart & Hands employs an unusual bottle closure, made of glass, called the Vinolok. This stopper eliminates the possibility of cork taint, which is rare but happens when natural corks are used.

The tasting room is small but staffed with knowledgeable wine lovers happy to pour samples. Heart & Hands' tasting room is open from Friday through Sunday unless you have a tasting appointment—see their website for details.

Heart & Hands produces approximately 2,000 cases per year.

Hosmer Estate Winery

The Hosmer vineyard, known as the Patrician Verona Vineyard, began in 1973 with the first planting of five acres of vines on the Hosmer family farm. These are some of the oldest vines on Cayuga Lake, planted by owners Cameron and Maren Hosmer. The Hosmers sold grapes to other producers for some years, then in 1985 decided to open Hosmer Winery. The current tasting room dates to 1990 (previously it was across Route 89, in the family garage). Today the vineyard, which remains at

the heart of Hosmers' approach to making fine wine, comprises 70 acres of vines: Pinot Noir, Cabernet Franc, Lemberger, Pinot Gris, Chardonnay, Riesling, Grüner Veltliner, and Sauvignon Blanc, along with some natives and hybrids—fifteen varieties in all.

Hosmer is fully an estate winery, producing wine only from the fruit of its own vineyards, which surround the winery and tasting-room buildings. They offer a nice range of dry white and red vinifera: Lemberger and Cab Franc in the reds, and Pinot Gris, Riesling, Chardonnay, Sauvignon Blanc, and Grüner Veltliner in the whites. Their Sauvignon Blanc, the only estate-grown Sauvignon Blanc on Cayuga Lake, is made in the New Zealand style—crisp and lemony—not surprising given winemaker Aaron Roisen's extensive experience making wine in New Zealand. Their Single Wheel Riesling is an interesting twist on the single-vineyard concept, with four distinct wines expressing the effects of terroir and the art of the winemaker. It is a dry wine intended to be made each year from the same vines. The goal here is to form a collection for vertical tasting from one vintage to the next. The wines designated First Spoke, Second Spoke, and Third Spoke are again single-vineyard, single-clone, and single-yeast productions but display the ability of the winemaker to produce dry (First), semi-dry (Second), and sweet (Third) Rieslings, and drive home the remarkable versatility of the Riesling grape. Chardonnay is made in two styles, lightly oaked (a combination of stainless-steel fermentation, around 70 percent, and oaked, the remaining 30 percent) and more fully oaked, the entire wine spending about nine months in the barrel. Their Chardonnay vines date to the early 1970s, a ripe old age for Finger Lakes vines. Hybrids and natives include a Cayuga White, and a few sweet Catawba and raspberry-infused wines. They have a Pinot Noir sparkling rosé and a Cayuga White sparkling wine, and their dessert wine is a fortified wine called Raspberry Royale, which is made with six pounds of local raspberries per gallon of wine—a base of Cayuga White, with raspberries and distilled spirits. The perfect beginning to a Kir Royale, if you have some sparkling white wine handy.

Timothy Hosmer, son of founders Cameron and Maren, now oversees the vineyard with his father. Tim also runs Benchmark Custom Vineyard Planting, employing GPS-guided planting machinery to get new vineyards up and running throughout the East Coast. Winemaker Aaron Roisen, who as mentioned above has extensive experience in New Zealand, also worked at Lamoreaux Landing and was assistant winemaker at Atwater Estate Vineyards before becoming head winemaker at Hosmer.

Hosmer produces about 9,000 cases of wine per year.

King Ferry Winery/Treleaven Wines

King Ferry, the oldest winery on Cayuga Lake's eastern shore—and still among the few—planted its first vines in 1984 on what had been the Treleaven dairy farm. Wanting to keep a connection to the past and the land, owners Peter and Tacie Saltonstall decided to name their wines

Treleaven in tribute to the land their vineyards occupied. The first plantings included Chardonnay, Riesling, Gewürztraminer, and Pinot Noir, and have since added Cab Franc, Vignoles, and Vidal.

King Ferry's signature focus is on Chardonnay, which they produce in various styles: Silver Lining, as we might guess, is a stainless-steel-only (no barrel fermentation) affair, producing a popular fresh, fruit-forward Chardonnay. Other offerings include Tacie's Chardonnay, the namesake of co-owner Tacie Saltonstall, which is aged eleven months in oak yet retains a light, Chablis-style crispness. Peter Saltonstall's favorite is the Reserve Chardonnay, produced more in the California style with more oak. Treleaven has some award-winning Riesling, produced dry, semi-dry, and a nice sweeter Wobbly Rock Riesling—introduced in 2015—which has become one of their best-selling wines. They also produce Gewurz, a sweet Vidal Blanc called Gilded Lily, and a blush wine, Saumon. They even offer a nice apple wine.

King Ferry / Treleaven's Pete Saltonstall plants the first vine in 1984.

On the red side they offer Cabernet Franc, Pinot Noir, and Merlot varietals as well as a Meritage (Bordeaux-style) blend that has garnered impressive awards. Their Melange is billed as a "red for white wine drinkers" and is made of two Cornell-developed red grapes with some Chardonnay added in.

King Ferry grows most of the grapes in Treleaven wines on the twenty-seven acres of vineyard surrounding the winery, and occasionally purchases grapes from other Finger Lakes vineyards. The vineyards themselves benefit from some unusual practices, including a technique called palissage, a vine-trellising method developed in Europe. Treleaven grapes are all hand-harvested.

King Ferry and the Saltonstall family are very community-minded and sponsor and support numerous charitable causes throughout the area.

The winemaker here is Lindsay Stevens, one of the relatively few women winemakers in the region. She is a Finger Lakes native and graduate of Cornell's oenology program.

King Ferry is on the larger side for a high-quality, mostly vinifera winery, at about 10,000 cases per year.

Knapp Winery

Knapp Winery is by Finger Lakes standards an old-line operation, founded in 1984 by Doug and Sue Knapp with vines that were planted in the late 1970s. When the Knapps retired in 2000, the winery was sold to Glenora owners Gene Pierce and Scott Welliver, who have maintained Knapp as very much its own winery. The winemaker here is Steve DeFrancesco (also winemaker at Glenora), but all wines are made on-site and most are estate wines, with a few exceptions.

Knapp is home to a number of "firsts"—the first mechanical grape harvester in the Finger Lakes, the first winery restaurant on Cayuga Lake, the first Cab Franc planted and vinified in the Finger Lakes, the first alembic pot-still in the Finger Lakes (used to make their distilled spirits), and the first Siegerrebe east of the Rocky Mountains—this grape is a twentieth-century hybrid creation from Germany, which makes a white wine somewhat like Gewürztraminer. (The Siegerrebe vines are still growing at Knapp and as of this writing the wine is still to come.)

Knapp has sixty-five acres, of which forty are planted in vines: Riesling, Cabernet Franc, Chardonnay, Lemberger, Sangiovese, Merlot, Baco Noir, Cayuga, Catawba, Seyval, Vignoles, and De Chaunac, as well as the Siegerrebe just mentioned.

Their list of wines is full without being too numerous. The dry whites include the usual Chardonnay, Riesling, and Gewürztraminer. They have a Pinot Gris and a Seyval Blanc as well as a rosé, typically a blend of Cab Franc and Pinot Noir. Their brut sparkling wine is a Prosecco-like blend of Cayuga White and Chardonnay, and very appealing. Semi-sweet whites include Riesling, Gewurz, Cayuga White, Vidal Blanc, and Vignoles as well as a blend called Pasta White. They have a range of sweet and fruit wines for the sweet-tooth wine lover, including the old standbys for the Finger Lakes, Niagara and Catawba. In the reds they offer Sangiovese, a rare grape in the Finger Lakes (Ventosa Vineyards also offers an estate Sangiovese, and Long Point produces one but not from Finger Lakes grapes), as well as excellent examples of Lemberger and Cabernet Franc. Rounding out the reds are Pinot Noir, Merlot, Cabernet Sauvignon, a Meritage blend, and the other side of their "Pasta" collection, the blend Pasta Red.

On the dessert side Knapp makes ice wines when Nature allows (and sometimes an iced version—see page 74 for the difference), including a rare Cab Franc ice wine.

Their alembic pot-still is imported from Portugal and creates the spirits for their brandy, port, vodka, and grappa, which goes into their Limoncello (lemon-flavored spirit) and Limencello (the lime version).

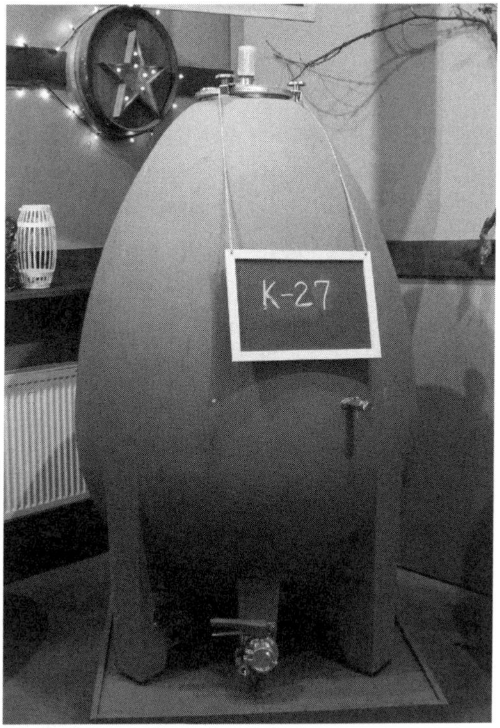

The concrete egg at Knapp. Fermentation in the egg gives an oak-like roundness to the wine without adding oak flavors.

One highly unusual and interesting winemaking method uses the odd-looking but intriguing "concrete egg," on display in the tasting room. As the chalkboard above it explains, the egg holds two hundred gallons of wine and originates in France. It was the find of owner Gene Pierce, who encountered it on a trip to France. Concrete eggs have been used in California winemaking since about 2003. The concrete is ideal for a wine like Chardonnay, where the winemaker might want to produce a crisp, fruity, non-oaky version of the wine. The concrete, in part because it "breathes" like an oak barrel does, imparts some roundness and softness to the mouthfeel of the wine but leaves out the oaky flavor. Knapp had made a Chardonnay with stainless-steel fermentation only but is transitioning to the concrete-egg method for their un-oaked Chardonnay. (Glenora also makes wine in eggs at their Seneca Lake winery.)

Knapp lies within the Cayuga Lake AVA and produces roughly 14,000 cases per year.

Long Point Winery

Sitting high on the slopes above Cayuga Lake's eastern shore is Long Point, one of the few wineries to be found on that side of Cayuga but well worth the visit. Long Point, founded in 1999 and therefore a relative newcomer to the Finger Lakes winemaking scene, is owned by Gary Barletta and his wife, Rosemary. Gary, a Syracuse native, had been an avid and successful home winemaker after inheriting winemaking equipment from his grandfather, who had made wine at home in the long-standing Italian tradition with then-young Gary at his side.

Long Point is best known for its dry wines, from dry Riesling to dry reds, but produces a full array of wines including the two Cabs, Franc and Sauvignon, Merlot, Chardonnay, Riesling, and Vidal Blanc, as well as a rosé called Ciera.

Unlike most other Finger Lakes wineries, Long Point has what is called a commercial winery license, as opposed to being a farm winery. The distinction effectively means that Long Point can produce wine using grapes from outside the Finger Lakes region, although such wines can't, and don't, have the words "New York" or "Finger Lakes" on their labels. The result for the wine lover is the opportunity to try locally made wine not ordinarily found in the Finger Lakes. Thus Long Point offers a Zinfandel, for example, one of the common, robust California reds. Reflecting Barletta's Italian heritage, Long Point also produces

Sangiovese, the principal grape in Chianti, as well as Barbera, a much-revered Italian wine grape. With the exception of Sangiovese, which is grown in limited quantities here, these grapes are (unfortunately) next to impossible to grow in the Finger Lakes, and Long Point brings them in from California. All the pressing and winemaking take place at the winery. Their excellent Pinot Grigio, which is grown extensively in Italy and elsewhere around the world, is an estate-grown product.

Long Point plants a modest eight acres of vineyards, growing Chardonnay, Riesling, Cabernet Franc, and Pinot Grigio. Other grapes are sourced locally and produced as Finger Lakes wine, or brought in from California as mentioned above.

The Long Point story is extensively chronicled in John C. Hartsock's excellent book *Seasons of a Finger Lakes Winery,* which details the Barlettas' story and looks at the day-to-day struggles and joys of the winemaking life. Highly recommended as an in-depth look at real-life winemaking, and as a peek inside the world of Finger Lakes wine producers.

Long Point's annual case quantity is about 2,500 per year.

Lucas Vineyards

The Lucas Vineyards story begins when Ruth Lucas and her tugboat-captain husband, Bill, moved from the Bronx to the western shore of Cayuga Lake, with three children in tow. There they resolved to start growing grapes, and on a sixty-acre parcel that had been a dairy farm they began clearing land and planting vines. By 1978 they had their first crop of grapes, which they sold to area wineries until 1980, when Ruth, the driving force behind Lucas Vineyards, decided to make a go of it making wine. The family has been doing so successfully ever since.

Lucas Vineyards was the first winery on Cayuga Lake. Ruth Lucas grew as a winemaker and vineyard owner, one of the few women to own a winery in the Finger Lakes, and in 1985 she teamed up with two other Cayuga Lake wineries to launch the Cayuga Wine Trail—this is the oldest wine trail in the United States, and of course still very active to this day.

Lucas now grows vinifera and hybrid grapes on about thirty-two acres. They grow some fourteen different varieties, the principal vinifera being Chardonnay, Riesling, Gewurz, Cab Franc, and Syrah. Hybrids include Vignoles, Vidal Blanc, Seyval Blanc, Noiret, and Cayuga White. All vinifera is handpicked; the hybrids are machine-harvested.

The Lucas wines come under three labels: Lucas, Tug Boat, and Nautie. The Lucas wines include all of the vinifera varietal wines such as Chardonnay, Riesling, Gewurz, Cab Franc, and Syrah, with hybrid varietals Cayuga White (also produced as a nice sparkling wine), Seyval Blanc, and Vignoles. Each of their varietals is an estate wine. Lucas-labeled blends range from dry to sweet and include a nice dry red blend, Dry Dock, combining Noiret and Baco Noir.

The Nautie series, playing on Lucas's nautical theme (Naut-ie), feature ladies in sailing garb on the labels. Look closely at the label on Miss Chevious—that's founder Ruth Lucas. Despite the playful label, which might lead to the assumption that this is a sweet wine, it's actually a dry white made from Chardonnay. The other two Nautie Misses—Miss Adventurous and Miss Behavin'—are sweet wines made from labruscas, Catawba and Niagara respectively.

Lucas's best-selling wine is an on-the-sweet-side red called Tug Boat Red. This is a blend of hybrid reds, mostly De Chaunac, but the blend varies from year to year as the goal is to produce the same wine with each vintage. Tug Boat Red makes up about half their total sales. Tug Boat White combines Cayuga, Vidal, and Vignoles.

In the dessert category they offer a pair of iced wines (see page 74 for a discussion of the difference between iced wines and ice wines), from Cab Franc and from Vidal.

Behind the current tasting-room building is a new winemaking facility, with tanks for fermentation and oak barrels for aging. They also have their own bottling operation. The winemaker at Lucas, taking over from Ruth, is her son-in-law Jeff Houck, who is married to Ruth's daughter Stephanie Lucas Houck, the VP of retail operations for the winery.

Lucas Vineyards produces about 26,000 cases per year, putting it on the larger side for a family-run operation. They have a nice range of well-made, well-priced wines for every taste.

Ports of New York

This winery is unlike any other covered in this book in that it makes a kind of fortified wine rarely if ever seen here in the Americas. Indeed, it should more properly be known as "European-Style Fortified Wines of New York," but somehow that name doesn't have the same ring to it. In any event, Ports of New York, which opened in May 2010, is the result of years of effort from owner and winemaker Frédéric Bouché, a French native with a long wine pedigree. His great-grandfather, Armand Bouché, opened an "urban winery" in the Normandy region of France in 1919, and Frédéric has patterned his operation on this winery style. The complexities of liquor licensure prevent Ports of New York from calling their wines ports or even fortified wines, so Frédéric has threaded the needle with the phrase "specialty wine." His is called Meleau and comes in two types, red and white.

Meleau—the name is a play on *miel*, French for "honey," and *eau*, as in *eau-de-vie*, both of which are used to craft the wines. These are fortified wines (wines to which distilled spirits have been added), but not as sweet, nor as high in alcohol, as typical ports. Rather these are wines common in France and elsewhere in Europe but almost never seen here—about 17 percent alcohol, and with a taste very much playing upon the wines from which they are made.

Bouché begins in the vineyard, which for Ports of New York is at Lamoreaux Landing's acreage on Seneca Lake. White Meleau uses mostly the hybrid grapes Muscat Ottonel and Vignoles; red Meleau is predominantly Cab Franc, with lesser amounts of Merlot and the hybrid Noiret. There the grapes are harvested in Bouché's presence and crushed immediately. He then transports the juice and (for the red) the skins, about five tons in all, to his winery in Ithaca. The juice and skins go immediately into fermentation tanks. About 15 percent of the white wine ferments on the skins, in open fermentation tanks, with the balance fermenting in a closed tank, off the skins. The open tank promotes oxidation, which for this kind of wine is good. Red wines stay on the skins through fermentation. Fermentation starts with inoculations of yeast, which Bouché grows himself in a solution of water and locally sourced honey that results in a viscous liquid that adds texture to the wine.

At about 8 percent RS and 7 percent alcohol—much more residual sugar and lower alcohol than typical table wine—fermentation is stopped; this is done by killing the yeast by adding distilled spirits (*eau-de-vie*), distilled from a Catawba wine Bouché makes in the winery. Fermentation takes only about ten days for both the whites and the reds.

After the eau-de-vie is added the wine sits in the tank for about six months, to allow the lees to fall and collect at the bottom of the tank; gradually the lees are removed.

Then it is time for the wine to move to the solera. The solera is a fairly complicated variation on the barrel room. A solera is composed of stacks of barrels in a triangular array. In the bottom row is the oldest wine; for Bouché that's at least four years old. Each row above it is a blend of successively younger wines combined with older. First about 25 percent of the wine in the bottom (oldest) row is removed and bottled. The wine in the upper barrels is moved down to the row below, eventually freeing up part of the top row, which gets the wine he has had in the tanks for six months.

The barrels themselves come from Lamoreaux Landing and are old, used, neutral barrels, at least ten years old. They are not intended to impart oak flavors, the way winemakers commonly wish to do. Instead Bouché needs the barrels for oxidation and evaporation. Oxidation helps give the wines their color and introduces flavors not imparted by the fruit, such as leather. "The wines need to be worked, " says Bouché. This is a much higher level of oxidation than would be desirable with other kinds of wine, and it can work because of the wines' higher levels of sugar and alcohol. Evaporation is important to concentrate the flavor of the wine. About three gallons per barrel per year is lost to evaporation, by design—about twelve hundred bottles of wine. (This evaporated wine is called the angel's share—and is at least deductible for excise tax purposes.) To promote evaporation he keeps the environment in the barrel room very dry. (Most barrel rooms, where you don't want evaporation, are kept or are naturally humid, so very little wine evaporates away.) If any barrels show signs of leakage, Bouché uses a steamer to re-swell the wood and seal them back up. The barrels themselves, if they're not moved, are kept full, and are sound to begin with, will last a long time. Barrels in French wineries making this type of wine are often three hundred years old.

These wines are drier and less alcoholic than typical ports from Portugal. They are still in the world of wines, at 17 percent alcohol; ports are 20 percent plus. In France wines such as those Bouché makes are common as an aperitif. In France one typically does not have a glass of table wine before dinner as is commonly done here. Instead one has a glass of fortified wine, along with some kind of hors d'oeuvres. The red wine he recommends with thin-sliced charcuterie or hearty cheese. The white, which may be perceived as sweeter but is actually less acidic, rather than more sweet, is great with pâté or an acidic cheese such as goat cheese. He has a friend who takes half a ripe cantaloupe, scores the flesh, then pours Meleau on top.

Because these wines are heavily oxidized during the winemaking, the wine does not change character after the bottle is opened as would a normal wine. Meleau wines retain their full flavors for at least six months after opening.

A new project—the energetic Bouché always seems to have a new project at the winery—is a greenhouse, which will house the only hydroponically grown vinifera grapes in the United States. The greenhouse will showcase vines of Cab Franc, Merlot, Noiret, Muscat Ottonel, and Vignoles, and the fruit will find its way into the wines, but these vines are intended more for esthetics than winemaking. The great majority of fruit will continue to be sourced at Lamoreaux Landing.

Ports of New York produces about 220 cases of wine per year, split more or less evenly between white and red, and sold in 500ml bottles. Bouché devotes exceptional care, patience, and skill to his wines, and they show it.

Sheldrake Point Winery

Sheldrake is a relatively young winery, founded in 1997 by Chuck Tauck and Bob Madill, on land that had been an orchard and dairy farm since 1850. Comprising 160 acres in all, of which 44 acres are planted with vinifera grapes, Sheldrake is nestled closer to Cayuga Lake than any other winery on the lake. This proximity allows the vineyard to take optimal advantage of the "lake effect" that we've seen so frequently in area wineries. At Sheldrake, because the lake is so close, and the offshore water so deep (some four hundred feet), the lake effect is accentuated, providing for a 170-day growing season—over two weeks longer than the hillsides nearby.

The first vines were planted in 1997 and the first wines, from a 2000 harvest, were released in 2001. Sheldrake is home to a careful selection of very well-crafted wines and is particularly noted for ice and dessert wines. The winery is strictly vinifera, all estate-grown.

The winemaker is Dave Breeden, with Dave Weimann as vineyard manager. The wines here are relatively few in number but are outstanding. They produce Riesling, Gewurz, and Chardonnay in the whites, and in reds Cab Franc, Gamay Noir (a rare grape for the Finger Lakes, which Sheldrake grows right next to the water), and Cab Sauvignon—the latter, again grown near the lake, produced as a varietal only when the fruit merits production. The Chardonnay is at times oaked with "estate" oak—with barrel staves from oak grown on the property. Rather than aging the wine in barrels, the staves are added to stainless-steel tanks. The result is a Chardonnay that tastes fresher, more like a Sauvignon Blanc. They also have a nice Cab Franc rosé.

As mentioned Sheldrake Point is noted for their dessert wines, and they do a Riesling ice wine every four years or so, when the winter weather cooperates. One bit of serendipity occurred in the winter of 2014–15, when they harvested a particularly large crop of ice-wine grapes, enough to fill two tanks. They moved one tank into the winery and produced their 2014 Ice Wine from this tank in the conventional manner. The other tank stayed outside during the winter. In April they tasted the contents and discovered it had begun a spontaneous fermentation—and was delicious. So the tank came indoors and produced their 2014 Wild Ferment Ice Wine, which they describe as "Nature's gift to Sheldrake Point." Winemaker David Breeden was quoted as saying, "This is a wine that will probably never happen again . . . Sometimes you just have to let a wine be what it wants to be, and this one is certainly quite special."

The Riesling world seemed to agree. Sheldrake's Wild Ferment Ice Wine won the Canberra International Riesling Challenge Competition, taking the prize over nearly five hundred Rieslings from around the world as Best Wine of the 2015 Challenge. A wine this rare does not come cheap—the 375ml bottle retailed for $100, and was worth every penny.

Sheldrake also produces a lovely apple dessert wine—this is an iced wine, with the water removed by freezing. Apples come from nearby orchards.

On the entry-level-wine side are two blends, a dry red, Luckystone Red, combining Cabernet Franc, Merlot, Cabernet Sauvignon, and Gamay Noir, and the corresponding Luckystone White, an off-dry blend of Chardonnay, Pinot Gris, Riesling, and Gewürztraminer.

Sheldrake Point Winery produces about 11,000 cases per year, and is well established among the highest-quality producers in the Finger Lakes.

Six Mile Creek Vineyard

Roger Battistella, the founder of Six Mile Creek, came to winemaking in a roundabout way. A professor of health policy and management at Cornell, Battistella took a sabbatical year in Europe in the 1970s and came home with the European outlook on wine as an integral part of the everyday table. Prior to this revelation, wine was not much in his culinary lexicon. Now it was.

He began making wine in his basement, and his winemaking skills increased. He became active in the American Wine Society chapter in Ithaca and added to his knowledge. By the early 1980s, still making wine in his basement, he finally felt he was a competent winemaker and was producing some two hundred gallons per year. In 1981 the land that would become Six Mile Creek went up for sale, and it seemed as if destiny had rung the doorbell. Battistella happened to live next door. So he bought the property, all twenty-four acres of it, and got to work.

He had his work cut out for him. He knew how to make good wine in his basement, but that's very different from operating a vineyard. Advisers at Cornell, from the Cooperative Extension office, told him the land was unsuited to grape growing and he should plant blueberries. Instead he planted vinifera, hybrid, and some labrusca grapes, and in the early years used them for home winemaking. Then in 1985 Roger and his wife, Nancy, took the plunge and decided to open a commercial winery.

He had a derelict dairy barn on the property that city officials insisted was hazardous and should be razed—but he had his heart set on using it as the tasting room. The tasting room you'll visit if you stop by on Route 79 is indeed the once-dilapidated dairy barn, now renovated and moved from its earlier location to the front of the property. Until 1995 the entire operation was downstairs; today the winery is downstairs and the tasting room on the ground floor.

Thanks to Battistella's vision for Six Mile Creek, Ithaca has its own very convenient, very friendly winery producing first-class wines, from grapes grown (at least partly) on the premises—and no blueberries. Six Mile Creek produces a total of seventeen different wines and grows these in the vineyard: Seyval, Vidal, Vignoles, Cayuga White, Muscat, Traminette, and Riesling.

All are whites. Until recently Chardonnay was also grown in the vineyard, but the vines could not handle the harsh temperatures and had to be pulled in 2014. Six Mile Creek's location is a blessing for visitors coming down Route 79 into Ithaca, but the distance from the lake is a handicap. Six Mile gets no lake-effect warming in winter, so growing grapes there has special challenges. For this reason Six Mile Creek grows no red-wine grapes, either.

However, like many other Finger Lakes wineries, Six Mile Creek augments its own grapes with fruit from other Finger Lakes vineyards, principally on Cayuga Lake. They make a well-rounded menu of both red and white wines, both vinifera and hybrids, with some native-grape offerings as well. Of special interest is their Seyval Blanc, which falls somewhere between a Pinot Gris, which is always pleasant but tends to lack complexity, and a Sauvignon Blanc, a wine with a much broader flavor characteristics. Their Vignoles, a popular Finger Lakes hybrid wine that tends to sweetness, is made in a drier style at Six Mile Creek, as is their Chardonnay. Six Mile Creek looks for more of a Chablis style in their Chardonnay, crisp and minerally, although they can (and often do) make a big, oaky, buttery Chardonnay more in the California style. Battistella has experimented widely with different barrel types and fermentation decisions (malolactic fermentation or not, for example) in their Chardonnays, resulting in a nice array of styles.

Battistella has always been a champion of blended wines, which of course account for many of the most important wines in the world, such as Bordeaux. Among the most popular and best-selling wines at

Six Mile Creek are blends known as Ithaca White and Ithaca Red. The White is a blend of hybrid Cayuga and vinifera Chardonnay. Red is predominantly the hybrid Marechal Foch, with about 10 percent of either Cabernet Sauvignon or Cabernet Franc for added tannins, and a bit of aging in oak. The goal with the "Ithacas" is to produce a consistent wine with similar flavor characteristics each year.

Another notable blend is called Quintessence, a Bordeaux-style blend of red vinifera. When a barrel of any of the three classic Bordeaux red wines—Cabernet Sauvignon, Merlot, or Cabernet Franc—seems particularly appealing, it's marked with a "Q," meaning it's destined to be used in Quintessence. With this wine Six Mile Creek strives to make a wine that is complex, dry, and interesting. Unlike the Ithaca Red and White, Quintessence will not be the "same" wine from one year to the next.

One of the offerings that really sets Six Mile Creek apart is their line of distilled spirits. They got into the distilling business when the Battistellas were vacationing with friends and fellow winery owners Doug and Sue Knapp in Italy, and admired the Italian version of distilled spirits. Knapp had already begun distilling wine into spirits and urged Battistella to give it a try. So he bought a twenty-five-gallon pot-still and made vodka and grappa. The results were a pleasant surprise, and one of their most popular offerings was born.

They've continued to make the spirits, including: Limoncello, Orangecello (both fruit-infused vodkas), gin, and their new best-selling spirit, Amore, an almond-and-other-nut-flavored Amoretto-style liqueur.

Although we tend to think of vodkas, gins, and other spirits as being made from sources other than grapes, all these can be made from any grapes. That is how it's done at Six Mile Creek, usually using either Cayuga or Seyval.

Update: Six Mile Creek was sold by the Battistellas in July 2015 to Mark and Amy Renodin. Paul King, the longtime assistant to Roger Battistella, is now the winemaker. Case quantity at Six Mile Creek is approximately 5,000 per year.

Swedish Hill Winery

The beginnings of Swedish Hill go back not quite as far as Dr. Frank, Walter Taylor, and others, but close enough—back to 1969, when Dick and Cindy Peterson started the winery as a part-time endeavor and built it, over the years, to a substantial enterprise with a total of three separate wineries in their stable. Swedish Hill (the name is a nod to the Peterson's Swedish heritage) is the largest, producing about 60,000 cases of wine per year. In addition the Peterson family owns Goose Watch Winery, opened in 1997 not far from Swedish Hill on Route 89 overlooking Cayuga Lake, and the Penguin Bay Winery on Seneca Lake (formerly called the Finger Lakes Champagne House), opened in 2005. Today, Swedish Hill is owned by Dave and Jean Peterson (Dave being the son of the founders). Dave, a viticulture PhD, serves as CEO.

Swedish Hill offers an extensive list of red and white wines from vinifera to hybrids to native-grape varieties, made in classic dry styles all the way to sweeter informal sipping wines. Grapes are sourced from four different farms totaling about eighty acres. In addition to vinifera still wines (Riesling, Gewurz, Pinot Grigio, and Chardonnay in the whites; Cab Franc, Pinot Noir, Lemberger, and a Bordeaux blend called Optimus in the reds), they have several different sparkling wines, including Naturel, a very pleasant blend of Chardonnay and Cayuga, and a rare sparkling Riesling. All the still wines are made at the Swedish Hill Winery in Romulus; the sparklers, including those labeled for Swedish Hill, are made at the "sister" winery, Goose Watch.

Another unusual offering here is Swedish Glogg, a red wine spiced with cinnamon, cloves, cardamom, and ginger, and typically served warm as a winter holiday treat. Swedish Hill also does some distilling and sells its own eau-de-vie, a form of brandy, and a port made from red wine fortified with the *eau-de-vie*.

A few wines are named in honor of Doobie, the miniature donkey who lives in the barn on the winery property. Smart Ass Red, a medium-dry red, is one good example. Tasting-room guests are invited to say hello to Doobie.

Swedish Hill is a significant presence in Finger Lakes winemaking and offers an unusually wide range of well-made wines.

Thirsty Owl Wine Company

Thirsty Owl has a well-balanced and well-made assortment of vinifera, hybrid, and native-grape wines. Opened in 2002, on 150 acres purchased the prior year by Ted Cupp, Thirsty Owl began with four wines and about twelve hundred cases. The original employee, Shawn Kime, is now head winemaker, and the company is headed up by Jon Cupp, Ted's son.

The vineyards extend all around the current winery and tasting room, with more recent plantings across the road. Most wines are estate-grown, with some grapes sourced from the vineyards near the winery that are not owned by Thirsty Owl. Included in the estate-grown selection is Malbec, a very unusual grape in the Finger Lakes, and grown on less than an acre sited mere steps from the edge of Cayuga Lake, the better to gain the warming lake effect to protect this typically warm-climate variety. The Malbec is not produced as a varietal but is included in a blend of three reds (Cab Sauv, Malbec, and Syrah).

Vinifera include Pinot Gris, Chardonnay, Gewürztraminer, and Riesling in the whites, and in the reds Pinot Noir, Syrah, and the blend of Cab Sauv, Malbec, and Syrah. Among the white hybrids are Vidal Blanc, and a Cayuga-Seyval blend; red blends include "Lot 99," combining Chancellor and Pinot Noir. Chancellor is also offered as a varietal. Their lightly oaked Chardonnay is oaked with barrel staves placed into the stainless-steel fermentation tank, rather than being aged more traditionally in an oak barrel.

On the dessert side Thirsty Owl has a very unusual, very pleasing ice wine made from Cabernet Sauvignon—this is the only Cab Sauv ice wine in the Finger Lakes. Although the wine gods sometimes intervene

The view at Thirsty Owl.

with weather that makes ice wine impossible, Thirsty Owl makes it when they can. The Cab Sauv ice wine has a brownish-pink tint and usually comes in at about 14 percent alcohol.

Also in the dessert category is their Vinte (meaning "twenty" in Portuguese), a port-style blend of Cab Sauv, Cab Franc, and Chancellor, plus distilled spirits, that is aged in oak for five and a half years. They have also recently introduced a hard cider named Fujac, a dry sparkling cider from various apple varieties grown at nearby Red Jacket Orchards.

Thirsty Owl overlooks one of the most impressive views of Cayuga Lake to be found anywhere. They produce in the area of 15,000 cases per year.

The name Thirsty Owl is at least partially explained on their label, which recites a legend of an owl that strikes a bargain to protect vineyards from birds and miscellaneous critters in exchange for wine. The owl is doing a sterling job.

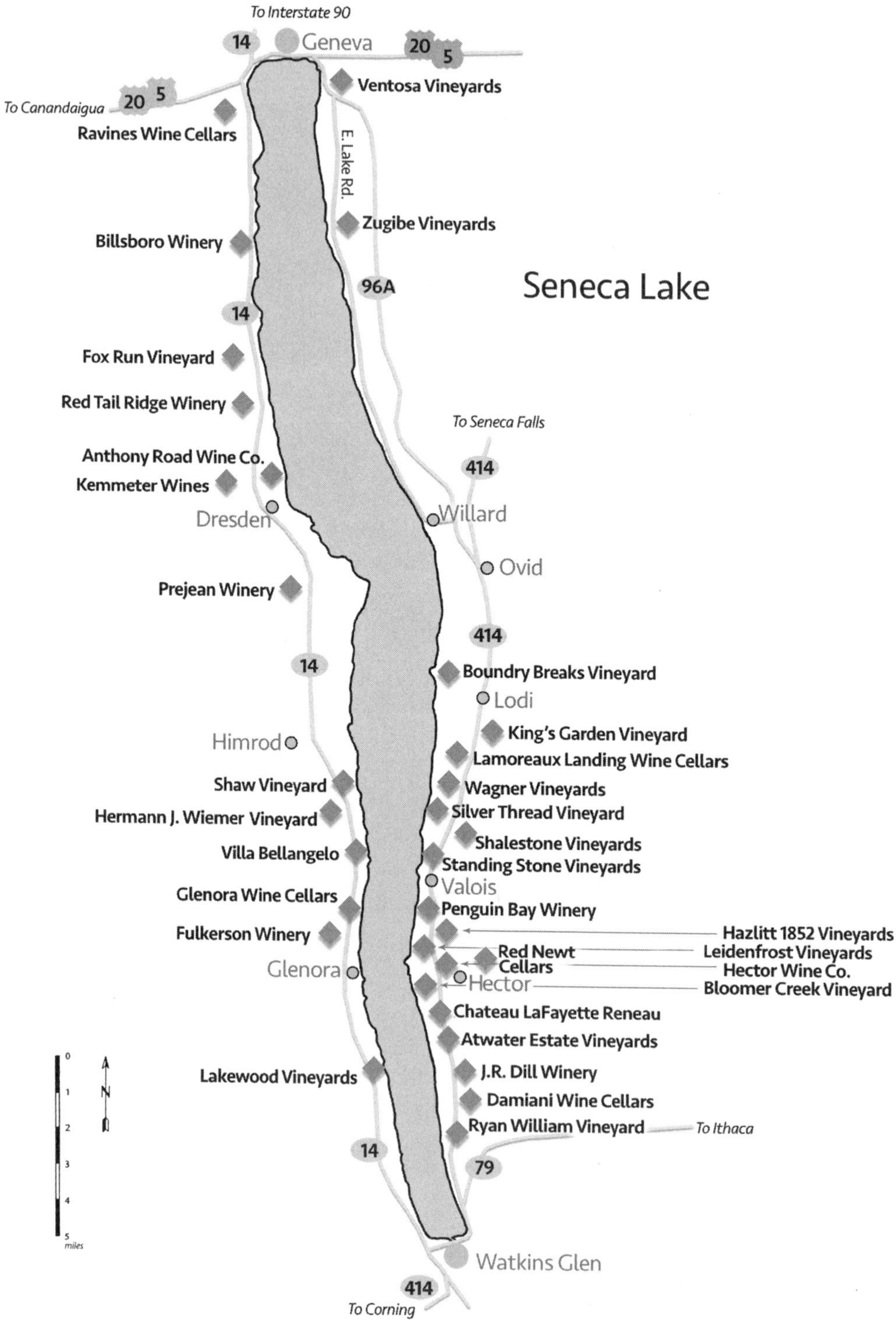
To Interstate 90
14
Geneva
20
5
Ventosa Vineyards
To Canandaigua
20
5
Ravines Wine Cellars
E. Lake Rd.
Zugibe Vineyards
Billsboro Winery
96A
Seneca Lake
14
Fox Run Vineyard
Red Tail Ridge Winery
To Seneca Falls
Anthony Road Wine Co.
414
Kemmeter Wines
Dresden
Willard
Ovid
Prejean Winery
414
14
Boundry Breaks Vineyard
Lodi
King's Garden Vineyard
Himrod
Lamoreaux Landing Wine Cellars
Shaw Vineyard
Wagner Vineyards
Hermann J. Wiemer Vineyard
Silver Thread Vineyard
Shalestone Vineyards
Villa Bellangelo
Standing Stone Vineyards
Valois
Glenora Wine Cellars
Penguin Bay Winery
Hazlitt 1852 Vineyards
Fulkerson Winery
Red Newt Cellars
Leidenfrost Vineyards
Hector Wine Co.
Glenora
Hector
Bloomer Creek Vineyard
Chateau LaFayette Reneau
Atwater Estate Vineyards
Lakewood Vineyards
J.R. Dill Winery
Damiani Wine Cellars
Ryan William Vineyard
To Ithaca
14
79
Watkins Glen
414
To Corning
0
1
2
3
4
5
miles
N

2 | *Seneca Lake Wineries*

SENECA LAKE is blessed with many of the best wineries in the Finger Lakes, and at times they are dotted along the roadside in numbers too great to count. This profusion of wineries is especially noteworthy in the so-called Banana Belt, the stretch of land running roughly from just north of Watkins Glen to Valois (that's *val-OYCE*). The Banana Belt enjoys a microclimate warmer than nearby acreage, especially near the lakefront, which can be extremely steep in spots. Thus not only is there a profusion of excellent wineries here—Damiani, Standing Stone, Shalestone, Atwater, LaFayette Reneau, and Red Newt, to name only a few—but the Belt also hosts one of the most important and productive vineyards in the Finger Lakes, Sawmill Creek Vineyard, owned and managed by Eric Hazlitt, the sixth generation of Hazlitts to grow grapes here. Sawmill Creek is the source of grapes for many of the top wineries in the region.

Beyond the Banana Belt, however, are many other wineries again among the very best in the Finger Lakes. Hermann J. Wiemer, Anthony Road, Fox Run, and Ravines are only a few of the wineries well outside the Banana Belt that are acknowledged as outstanding Finger Lakes producers.

Anthony Road Wine Company

Anthony Road began in 1973 when Ann and John Martini came to Yates County to purchase a hundred acres overlooking Seneca Lake and plant a vineyard. Early harvests consisted of hybrids, which were sold to Taylor and other New York State wineries. In 1990 they launched the winery Anthony Road, named simply enough for the road you turn down from Route 14 to get to the winery driveway. In the years since the early-1973 plantings of hybrids, they have replaced the hybrid vines with vinifera, keeping only the Vignoles. Today about forty-five acres of the Martini Vineyard grows grapes for Anthony Road, with about 40 percent of their harvest sold to quality Finger Lakes producers such as Heart & Hands and Kelby James Russell for his signature label at Red Newt. Peter Martini, son of Ann and John, is the vineyard manager and also oversees the nearby Young Vineyard on Nutt Road, also about forty-five acres, and also producing fruit for Anthony Road. In the community spirit, Anthony Road donates two and a half acres of the Martini Vineyard for use by students at Cornell's Grape Program for research on grapes and viticulture methods as well as Finger Lakes Community College viticulture students to obtain hands-on vineyard experience.

The winemaker is Peter Becraft, who joined Anthony Road in 2006 and apprenticed under then-head-winemaker Johannes Reinhardt, who remains a consulting winemaker as he develops his own winery, Kemmeter, across the road (described below). Becraft started at Anthony Road almost by accident, meeting Reinhardt in the tasting room and eventually signing up to help with the fall harvest. Things progressed from there, and when Reinhardt fulfilled his dream of finding the right vineyard property in 2013, Becraft became head winemaker.

Wines include an un-oaked Chardonnay, Gewurz, Riesling in dry, semi-dry, and semi-sweet styles, plus the "Art" series of Riesling, so named because the label features one of Ann Martini's attractive paintings; the Art Riesling is a spontaneous fermentation, using natural yeasts. They also have a Pinot Gris, sometimes with an unusual barrel-fermented treatment, and a Vignoles, presented both semi-dry and as a dessert wine. Reds feature a Cab Franc–Lemberger blend first developed by Johannes Reinhardt; this is a delicious wine that dovetails the soft fruit of the Lemberger with the tannin of the Cab Franc. Pinot Noir is excellent here but is produced only when the fruit develops properly so it is not an every-vintage offering. They also offer Merlot, and in rosé they have a Cab Franc.

Other wines include blends: The Devonian series consists of light, dry wines blended from vinifera and hybrids in both red and white wines. The Devonian wines are concocted each year from fully fermented and aged wines and then blind-tasted to make the most appealing combination. Their series of "Tony" wines—Tony's Red, White, and Blush—are named for a family friend, Tony Castelluzzo, whose profile appears on the label. These are light, semi-sweet wines made from hybrid grapes, and in a style favored by Mr. Castelluzzo.

Owner John Martini deserves some sort of award for trekking to New York City's Green Market, at 17th and Broadway, virtually every weekend since the mid-1990s. This is a practice he still maintains, bringing a taste of the Finger Lakes to the great unwashed in Manhattan. Perhaps because of the visibility his trips have garnered, the New York Yankees approached Anthony Road asking if the winery could produce a Yankees-themed wine, and the Yankees Reserve Dry Riesling, sporting the familiar team logo, is the result.

Anthony Road produces around 15,000 cases of wine per year, putting it at the more prolific end of top-quality producers in the region.

Atwater Estate Vineyards

The Atwater vineyard occupies some of the oldest vine-planted ground in the Finger Lakes, having been planted as vineyard since the early years of the twentieth century. Some Catawba vines, still grown on the property, and still producing wine grapes, date from the 1920s. Situated squarely in the Banana Belt on the southwestern edge of Seneca Lake, Atwater has prime territory for growing grapes and produces outstanding wines.

Like just about all Finger Lakes vineyards, the vineyard we now know as Atwater had been a strictly native-variety affair in the early years, producing Concord and Catawba and other native grapes. In 1970 a wine-business entrepreneur named Bill Moffett bought the property and began plantings of vinifera and hybrids. These did well and the plantings expanded. In 1980 Moffett sold the land to Ed and Joanne Grow, who had decided to seize the opportunity afforded by the Farm Winery Act of 1976. The Grows opened the Rolling Vineyards Farm Winery, producing estate wines from the land for the first time, and expanded the plantings to include Riesling, Gewürztraminer, and Vidal Blanc. Rolling Vineyards closed its doors in 1991, but not before sharing top honors with Wagner in the first Governor's Cup, the highest state award for New York State wines. Although the Rolling Vineyards winery was gone, the vines continued to be cultivated for sale to other wineries until 1999, when local businessman and current owner Ted Marks purchased the vineyard and established Atwater Estate Vineyards. Aided by then-son-in-law Phil Hazlitt, Atwater was soon making very high-quality wines. Since 2003 the winemaking duties at Atwater have been the charge of winemaker Vinny Aliperti, who focuses on carefully tended, crisp, fruit-forward wines and makes some of the best wines the Finger Lakes has to offer. Aliperti is also owner and winemaker of Billsboro Winery, profiled elsewhere in this book, but making the Billsboro-labeled wines here at the Atwater facility.

About 85 percent of Atwater wine is estate-grown, taking advantage of their prime vineyard location extending almost to the edge of Seneca Lake. The balance of their grapes come typically from vineyards within a few miles' distance, such as the Navone Vineyard Dry Riesling, sourced from Navone Vineyard about a quarter mile north along Route 414.

Atwater features some unusual wines, like a carbonated Riesling called Riesling Bubble and a similar Pinot Noir rosé called Pinot Bubble. (The carbonation process requires specialized winery equipment and thus is not done here: Other wineries in the region handle the carbonation for these wines.) Also notable is their Riewürz, a blend of (you guessed it) Riesling and Gewürztraminer, which was first produced as an experiment in 2004 when Atwater found it had too little fruit of both varieties to make varietals. After a few years' hiatus when the wine was not made, popular demand brought it back in 2009 and it is now made just about every vintage year. Their Chardonnay tends to be very much in the cool-climate, Chablis style, using fruit from their oldest vinifera vines, planted in 1978. Among their reds are a Blaufränkisch (aka Lemberger, but Atwater prefers this original Austrian name), a wine in limited production with less than an acre planted, and a Syrah. This is among the few Finger Lakes wineries producing Syrah, which needs the very best of the lake-effect warmth to grow successfully here.

Atwater produces a *méthode champenoise* wine more or less every other year, generally fewer than three hundred cases. They had special success with their 2010 Cuvée Brut, a fifty-fifty blend of Chardonnay and Riesling, which won a ninety-one-point score and was named the "Best US Sparkling Wine" by *Wine & Spirits* in December 2015.

Testament to the high standards at Atwater, and the generous spirit of owner Ted Marks, is the remarkable stream of excellent winemakers who have learned or refined their craft at Atwater. These include Aaron Roisen, winemaker at Hosmer; Tom Higgins, who founded Heart & Hands Winery on Cayuga Lake; Justin Boyette at Hector Wine Company; and Kris Mathewson at Bellwether Winery.

Besides the specific wines mentioned above, Atwater offers Riesling, Gewurz, and Chardonnay in the vinifera whites and Seyval Blanc, Vidal Blanc, Villard Blanc, Vignoles, and the Cornell-originated Cayuga White in the hybrids. On the red side they have the aforementioned Lemberger and

Syrah, plus Cabernet Franc, Cabernet Sauvignon, and Pinot Noir, hybrids Chancellor, Chelois, Marechal Foch, and Noiret, and the native Catawba.

Atwater's production level ranges between 5,000 and 8,000 cases per year, not including the Billsboro wines.

Billsboro Winery

The original Billsboro Winery (the name comes from the town of Billsboro, along Route 14 in the northwest corner of Seneca Lake, which is easy to miss) was founded by Bob Pool and Jennifer Morris in 1999. Current owners Vinny and Kim Aliperti purchased the twenty-eight-acre property in 2007. Winemaker Vinny is also the winemaker at Atwater Estate Vineyards (discussed above) and indeed all Billsboro wines are made at Atwater, on the eastern side of Seneca Lake. Unlike Atwater, which true to its name is predominantly an estate-wine operation, the fruit from Billsboro is sourced mostly from Sawmill Creek, Leidenfrost, and to a lesser extent Atwater Vineyards.

Vinny Aliperti began his winemaking career making wine in Long Island, apprenticing under winemaker Roman Roth at Wolffer Estate. In 2000 the Alipertis moved to the Finger Lakes and Vinny worked at Hermann J. Wiemer Vineyard—his first exposure to, and a good place to learn about, Riesling. Shortly afterward he took over as winemaker at Atwater, and several years thereafter, with the blessing of Atwater chief Ted Marks, the Alipertis purchased Billsboro.

The focus here is mostly on dry, fruit-driven wines in the cool-climate style, relatively low in alcohol, and not heavily oaked. Aliperti tends toward experimentation with winemaking, such as his on-the-skins fermentation of Chardonnay or his barrel-fermented dry Riesling, which is exclusively barrel-fermented for eight months in neutral French oak (this wine scored ninety points from *Wine Enthusiast*).

There are not a lot of wines here but what they do is done exceptionally well, focusing on single-vineyard, classic vinifera varietals.

Whites include Riesling and Chardonnay, and the blend Kashong White (*kashong* is a Seneca word meaning "river with two branches"), which combines Cayuga White and Vidal Blanc. On the red side they offer Cabernet Franc, Cabernet Sauvignon, Pinot Noir, and Syrah—all when the fruit is right. They also produce a rosé, which tends to sell out quickly, and a dessert wine, either a late-harvest or, when the wine gods see fit, an ice wine.

Billsboro's appealing label design features what looks like a lemon slice but is actually a cross section of a Cabernet Franc vine.

In warmer months Billsboro operates a satellite tasting room on the other side of Seneca Lake, at the Rose Hill Mansion in Waterloo.

Clearly these are handcrafted, carefully made wines. Production is quite modest, at around 2500 cases per year, but quality is high.

Bloomer Creek Vineyard

Bloomer Creek emphasizes traditional vinifera wines produced from small batches of estate-grown grapes, meticulous hand-tending in the vineyard, and the absolute smallest possible intervention in the winery. In many ways the owners, the husband-and-wife team of Kim Engle and Debra Bermingham, have found kindred spirits in the natural-wine movement, a new wave centered mostly in Europe that promotes sustainable vineyard management, hand-picking and cluster-thinning the grapes, indigenous yeast fermentation, little to no fining (in which a neutral substance, often egg white, is added to wine to help clarify it, then removed), little to no filtering, and few to no sulfites—all practices that Bloomer Creek has been employing for some time.*

Kim Engle came to winemaking with a sort of revelation in 1978, while a Cornell student with a part-time job in a Cayuga Lake vineyard. The life of the vineyardist suited him well, and he went on to study winemaking at California State in Fresno (Cornell had no oenology program at the time). He and Debra married soon thereafter and in the mid-1980s they bought a farm and some vineyard land on the western shore of Cayuga Lake, and began planting grapes. The vineyards progressed slowly and in 1999 they launched Bloomer Creek Vineyard. (The creek known as Bloomer Creek runs behind their farmhouse.)

The ten-acre vineyard is divided in two sections, known as the Auten Vineyard and the Morehouse Road Vineyard. One intriguing feature distinguishing these two is the planting direction: Auten is planted north–south, so the grapes get sun from both sides, while Morehouse Road is planted east–west, keeping one side of the grape clusters out of direct sunlight. The subtleties of different ripening that result make for interesting and delicious differences in the wines.

In 2012 they added a third parcel of land, which they call the Barrow Vineyard, on Mathews Road about a mile from the tasting room and winery on the eastern shore of Seneca Lake. This vineyard had been planted in Catawba and was abandoned for some thirty years. After a lot of work clearing out vines, posts, trellis wire, and thirty years of weeds, they have a fresh vineyard planted, for now, with four acres of Riesling. Still planned are another four acres each of Cab Franc and Chenin Blanc.

All told, Bloomer Creek grows Chardonnay, Riesling, Gewurz, Grüner Veltliner, Chenin Blanc, Cab Franc, Merlot, and Pinot Noir. Essentially this is an estate-only winery, although in extreme cold-weather years, if an important crop is totally knocked out, they will purchase grapes from nearby vineyards. They produce varietals (single-grape wines) of

** One of the central exponents of the natural-wine movement is French wine blogger Isabelle Legeron, whose website (www.thatcrazyfrenchwoman.com) includes much more information.*

all of these except the Merlot, which is included in their blend known as White Horse. The winemaking, as noted above, is intensely hands-off. They vinify in very small lots, doing individual fermentations that can often last six months or more, and produce as little as forty cases of a particular wine.

Riesling is one particular focus, with grapes picked three times in the German tradition. The first-harvest Riesling results in a Kabinett style; second harvest yields a Spätlese. Their late-harvest Riesling is sweet but refreshing, not syrupy. In keeping with the natural-wine philosophy and the traditions of European cool-climate wines, they allow botrytis (a late-season fungus that intensifies grape flavors) to develop and concentrate the grapes.

Bloomer Creek's signature red is White Horse, a nod to the famed Bordeaux label Château Cheval Blanc. White Horse is a seventy-thirty blend of Cab Franc and Merlot, with a refreshingly low alcohol level—the way Bordeaux used to be—of about 12.5 percent.

Reds at Bloomer Creek are aged from six months to a year, depending upon the aims of the winemaker. They are at pains to avoid over-oaking a wine, with their youngest barrel coming in at twelve years old. (The fresher the barrel, the more oak flavor is imparted to the wine.) In years when they are not able to get adequate ripening in the vineyard, they make a Cab Franc as a *vin d'été* (summer wine), which involves whole-cluster fermentation of the grapes. The *vin d'été* usually includes some Gamay, the traditional Beaujolais grape. Although unlike Beaujolais this is not a true carbonic maceration, it still produces a fruity, light, Beaujolais-style wine that has proved very popular and is among the favorites of Assistant Winemaker Katy Koken, who has been part of the Bloomer Creek winemaking team since graduating from Cornell in 2011, and before that was a part-time cellar assistant.

Besides the *vin d'été*, Bloomer Creek's more informal wine is a blend called Edelzwicker that combines Riesling, Gewurz, Cayuga White, and others. This is a bistro-style wine common in Alsace.

Bloomer Creek is quite small in production, about 2,000 cases, and the tasting room is open sparingly—one weekend day per week. (Check their website for details.) The winery has achieved the kind of success and praise in various wine publications that would be more common for a larger winery—a testament to the rewards of sticking to principles.

Boundary Breaks Vineyard

Boundary Breaks is a unique proposition in Finger Lakes winemaking: It is a vineyard, only a vineyard, yet makes wine. How? The key is collaboration.

Boundary Breaks owner Bruce Murray is an entrepreneur and veteran of newspaper and electronic publishing who hit upon a novel idea: Focus on producing the best possible fruit and take advantage of the deep experience and talent of area winemakers to make the wine. Murray is a Syracuse native, passionate about making the best wine he can.

Murray found acreage at the northern quadrant of Seneca Lake's east side and has planted about eighteen acres, mostly Riesling but also Gewurz, Cab Franc, Merlot, and Cab Sauv. The vineyard is flanked on both sides by deep channels, called breaks, at the boundary of the property, hence the name on the label. First plantings were in 2008. Murray is serious about soil preparation, the best soil being a prerequisite for the best grapes. The soil in his acreage was ripped down four feet, which anyone who has planted even a vegetable garden in the rock-strewn Finger Lakes has to admire. This extensive soil loosening helps the vines root deeply. Next was the installation of drainage tile to keep out excess moisture during rainy spells. The vineyard benefits from lake-effect warming—a cold snap in the winter of 2015–16 had some nearby fields at eighteen degrees below zero Fahrenheit; Murray's vineyard saw a still-brisk but not fatal seven below.

All this was expensive and laborious, but worth it—Boundary Breaks has come seemingly from nowhere to rank among the best producers of Riesling in the Finger Lakes. And Riesling is, for now, all that they produce. A tasting at BB will take you through several outstanding wines, ranging from dry to semi-dry to a Spätlese-style sweeter Riesling—a true "short course" in what can be done with this grape. All are single-vineyard, small-batch wines. Murray makes arrangements with prominent area winemakers and wineries to produce the wine—he supplies the fruit and buys the fermentation tanks, then collaborates with the winemakers to establish the style he is looking for. The first vintage at Boundary Breaks was 2011.

Overseeing the vineyard at Boundary Breaks is Kees Stapel, who had worked at Sheldrake. The vineyard practices are rigorous and exacting. The vines are trained on a Scott Henry trellis system, the particulars of which are beyond the scope of this book, but suffice it to say it is expensive to set up and labor-intensive to manage. Cluster-thinning, leaf removal, and careful by-hand harvesting are also the rule here.

As of this writing a number of changes are afoot at Boundary Breaks, including a new tasting room (tastings are by-appointment-only until the tasting room opens) and a wider selection of offerings, including a red wine. Murray is looking for the red that he hopes will become the "signature" red grape for the Finger Lakes, the way Riesling is the signature white. This red may be Cab Franc, maybe Lemberger, maybe an outlier like Saperavi. Whatever wine he makes from Boundary Breaks fruit, Murray has set a high bar—to compete with the best wines in the world. With the wines at Boundary Breaks so far, he is well on his way.

Annual production at the winery is on the increase but currently stands at around 5,000 cases.

Chateau LaFayette Reneau

Although this may sound like an extension of an esteemed French Bordeaux label, Chateau LaFayette Reneau is very much an all-Finger Lakes affair. Founders Dick and Betty Reno bought a multipurpose farm in 1984 on 140 acres of what they perceived was prime potential vineyard acreage square in the Banana Belt of Seneca Lake's southeastern shore. A visit to the tasting room reveals what the farm looked like at the time; photos circulating on the display screen show the decrepit state of the old threshing barn. This barn became the present tasting room and (belowdecks) the winery, but only after quite a bit of love and effort on the part of the Renos.

The name for the winery comes from Dick Reno's grandfather William LaFayette Reneau (Reno is evidently a name easier for the American eye to make out). Today about fifty-seven acres are planted in grapevines, extending downslope from the winery toward the lake, bordered by Atwater on the south and some outbuildings on the north side. (More acreage is available and may be planted soon.) All their vinifera wines are estate wines, produced from their own grapes, and all winemaking and bottling operations are here as well. LaFayette Reneau offers most of the basic Finger Lakes vinifera: both Cabs (Franc and Sauvignon), Pinot Noir, Merlot, and Syrah (one of the few Syrahs made in the region) among the reds and Riesling, Chardonnay, and a Vidal Blanc in the whites. All are excellent, well-made wines. The Chardonnay is offered in two styles, the cold-climate Chablis style and an oakier, buttery California style. And like many other wineries they make a rosé, typically from Pinot Noir. LaFayette Reneau also has some dry and semi-dry blends of hybrids and vinifera, and some sweet wines made with labruscas (Concord, Niagara, and Catawba Mist) with fruit sourced elsewhere in the Finger Lakes. Dessert wines include late-harvest Vidal Blanc and Riesling.

The Renos sold the winery to Glenora's Gene Pierce and Scott Welliver in 2013, contemplating retirement, but sadly Dick Reno passed away the next year. Pierce and Welliver, who in addition to Glenora also own Knapp Winery on Cayuga Lake, are keeping the LaFayette Reneau label as an independent operation with its own distinguished identity. LaFayette Reneau produces around 20,000 cases per year.

Damiani Wine Cellars

Damiani is a relatively young winery, with their first wines being offered in 2004. The winery began when owners Lou Damiani (who works at Cornell) and Phil Davis (a logger by profession), sharing a love of wine, determined to try their hand at making it. They planted their first grapes in 1997 in what is now Davis Vineyard and Damiani Vineyard, both near the tasting room. In 2004 they had their first vintage, offering a Riesling and six different reds.

They continued building the business with Damiani doing the winemaking and Davis growing the grapes, although the wine in the bottles has always been made in close collaboration. In 2009 a third partner, Glenn Allen, joined the winery to focus on the business end, and in 2010 a winemaker, Phil Arras, joined the team to work alongside Lou Damiani in the winery. Damiani sources from three different vineyards (a soon-to-be-fourth is quite new and still being planted) sprinkled along Route 414, all very close to the winery itself, totaling about forty acres. The namesake Damiani Vineyard showcases Merlot, with Cab

Franc and Syrah a close second. (Again Syrah, an unusual grape in the Finger Lakes, can be grown in vineyards like this one, in the Banana Belt on Seneca.) Each plot here is small, from one-half to two and a half acres, forcing close attention to each vine. The Davis vineyard, also on Seneca's eastern shore, is a five-and-a-half-acre site growing mostly Pinot Noir but also Merlot, Cabernet Sauvignon, Sauvignon Blanc, and Riesling. On western Cayuga Lake is the Sunrise Hill Vineyard, independently owned and farmed by Bob and Cathy Ruiz, which again features reds, mostly Lemberger and Pinot Noir.

Viticulture at Damiani stresses letting the vines struggle—and properly so, as grapevines need to force their roots into the mineral-rich ground to yield quality dry-wine fruit. Hand-harvesting, careful canopy management, and limited fruit-per-vine are all standards here.

As one might guess from the grapes described above, reds are the focus at Damiani, although not exclusively. Their MC^2 wine—the "M" for "Merlot" (around 50 percent) and the "C^2" for the two "Cabs," Franc and Sauvignon (around 25 percent each, the blend depending on the year)—is their red blend with a soft, Merlot feel. Aged in neutral barrels for eight months, and first offered in the 2012 vintage, this has proved a very popular wine. Their Bordeaux-style Meritage puts the more tannic Cabs at the front in a close-to-even blend of Cabernet Franc and Cabernet Sauvignon, with smaller amounts of Merlot. Most of their wines are estate-grown but, like many other wineries, they do purchase grapes from other growers when they are unable to source what they need from their own vineyards. One common source is the Sunrise Hill Vineyard on Cayuga Lake. And like others, Damiani offers single-vineyard selections from Davis, Sunrise Hill, Sawmill Creek, and Damiani vineyards.

While we generally prefer to de-emphasize the ubiquitous point system of evaluating wines, it is worth noting that *Wine Spectator*'s James Molesworth awarded Damiani's 2010 Reserve Cabernet Sauvignon the highest rating to date for a Finger Lakes red wine—a score of ninety.

Red isn't the *only* wine here, by any means. Their Bollicini is a Prosecco-like sparkler made from Cornell-hybrid Cayuga, Pinot Noir, Chardonnay, and Pinot Meunier, a rare grape in the Finger Lakes, which is typically used in French champagne. Damiani also sometimes offers a brut sparkling white, which is a more or less even blend of Chardonnay and Pinot Meunier.

Wines are mostly vinifera—Riesling, Pinot Grigio, Sauvignon Blanc, and Chardonnay in the whites, and Pinot Noir, Merlot, Cabernet Franc, Cabernet Sauvignon, Syrah, and Lemberger in the red varietals. In addition to the blends mentioned above they have a red blend called simply Vino Rosso that features hybrids Marechal Foch and Rougeon in addition to Merlot.

The wines themselves are made in the winery down the slope on Peach Orchard Road, not far from the current tasting room on Route 414, which opened in 2010. All told Damiani produces approximately 8,000 cases per year, which puts it in the not-too-small-but-not-too-big "Goldilocks" range, and typical wines are produced in amounts fewer than five hundred cases. Quality vinifera red wine, crafted carefully and expressive of the Finger Lakes, is the goal here, and Damiani succeeds admirably.

J. R. Dill Winery

Stop by J.R. Dill Winery on Seneca Lake and you'll likely meet Jeff Dill himself pouring at the appealing tasting bar, which is inlaid with a collection of Seneca Lake glass, assembled over a forty-year span by Jeff's mother, Jackie. Much of this glass is older than J.R. himself, who began making wine in his parents' basement as an eighteen-year-old. The hobbyist winemaker got more serious as the years passed and the result was the opening of J.R. Dill Winery in 2009. Dill's Finger Lakes wine pedigree dates back to his grandfather, H.R. Dill, who worked the Finger Lakes vineyards at the turn of the twentieth century.

Dill sources his grapes from Seneca Lake vineyards as much as possible, but the winery has no vineyards of its own. Winemaking has been done exclusively on-site since 2013. The wines are tailored in scope and the emphasis tends toward reds, with an interesting and unusual De Chaunac varietal being among their best-selling wines. (De Chaunac is a hybrid named for Canadian wine pioneer Adhémar de Chaunac.) The grape also appears in their blend DeFranc, with Cab Franc, and in Lake Glass Red, a blend of De Chaunac and the rare Cornell hybrid Geneva Red. Plans are afoot for another red hybrid, Marechal Foch, to be made as a varietal as well. Red vinifera include a Cabernet Sauvignon and a Merlot. On the white side their "house" white, Lake Glass White, can be a blend of Chardonnay with other grapes or sometimes pure Chardonnay. They also offer Rieslings and the hybrid Cayuga White in both still and sparkling styles. The sweet-wine fan will be happy with their Jabber-Waulkie wines, done as a blush, a white, and a sparkler.

J.R. Dill is still a young winery but is making some interesting wines you won't find elsewhere. There is a friendly, upbeat energy to the tasting room that well rewards a visit.

J.R. Dill produces in the region of 5,000 cases per year.

Fox Run Vineyards

Fox Run is a significant and important producer of Riesling and Chardonnay, and offers excellent examples of Lemberger, Pinot Noir, and Merlot as well as a Meritage (Bordeaux-style) red, a blanc de blancs (all-Chardonnay) sparkling wine, and fortified ports. Fox Run has been around for a while—the first planting of grapes was in 1984, and the nineteenth-century dairy barn was converted to a winery in 1993. The present tasting room and café space was completed in 2001.

Roughly 80 percent of their wines are estate-grown, from the fifty-five acres of vineyards extending on all sides of the winery building. Fox Run is intensely committed to exploring the terroir of their property, which lies along the ancient shoreline of what is known in the paleo-geology world as Lake Dana, the vast precursor to modern-day Seneca Lake. The ancient lakeshore left behind well-drained loam over shale and sandstone, perfect for growing Riesling. Fox Run's Geology series of Rieslings looks to explore the possibilities offered by the soil, with juice from specific acreage vinified in three distinct styles.

Fox Run is owned by founder Scott Osborn, John Kaiser manages the vineyard (Kaiser oversaw the original 1984 vineyard planting), and the winemaker is Peter Bell, who came to Fox Run in 1995 after five years as head winemaker at Dr. Konstantin Frank Vinifera Wine Cellars. Fox Run's Riesling forms one-third of the tripartite Tierce Riesling, produced with Rieslings from Anthony Road and Red Newt. (Tierce is discussed on page 149.) Riesling is an important commitment here, with at least nine different Riesling wines, but they also offer outstanding examples of Chardonnay and a variety of reds, including a Cab Franc–Lemberger blend first developed by Anthony Road's Johannes Reinhardt. Lemberger (aka Blaufränkisch) has been produced at Fox Run since 1997, with the first vines planted in 1995, putting them over twenty years old. Fox Run's five and a half acres of Lemberger make up the largest planting of the grape in New York State. All the Fox Run vines are spaced six feet apart; yield is a low three tons per acre. Vinification is guided by a minimal-intervention approach, with as little filtering as possible, and after tank fermentation most red wines are racked into some combination of French, American, and/or Hungarian oak barrels, where they will age anywhere from eight to eighteen months.

The vineyards at Fox Run.

In addition to the vinifera wines Fox Run produces a range of sweeter hybrids, including a Traminette, the Cornell-developed hybrid of Gewürztraminer. Also on the menu are ports, made from grape juice that has not quite turned into wine, which is then blended with distilled spirits and aged in oak. These include a ruby port, blended young and not aged for long, and the more complex, longer-aged tawny port. Hedonia, a relatively new experiment, is a white port made from Traminette grapes.

Owner Scott Osborn is also a devotee of garlic, so Fox Run hosts the annual August extravaganza of all-things-garlic, the Glorious Garlic Festival. This popular event brings ten thousand or more garlic fans to the winery.

Fox Run produces about 15,000 cases per year and is unquestionably a must-visit for any vinifera enthusiast.

Fulkerson Winery

Fulkerson Winery began production of wine in 1989, but its Finger Lakes roots extend much farther into the past. In 1805, well before the Reverend William P. Bostwick rode into Hammondsport, Caleb Fulkerson left the relative civilization of Somerville, New Jersey, to come to the wilds of western Seneca Lake, where he began farming. Caleb died in 1848 and his farmer-descendants continued to tend the Fulkerson land, introducing a limited amount of grapes as early as the 1830s, but it wasn't until the sixth generation, with Sayre Fulkerson, who started planting grapevines in earnest in the 1970s, that the Fulkerson Winery started to take root. Their first vintage was in 1989.

Fulkerson offers a wide range of the usual Finger Lakes wines—Riesling, Cabernet Franc, and a selection of sweeter native-grape sipping wines. More unusual are a sweet Moscato, a slightly fizzy (*frizzante* is the proper term), low-alcohol wine common in Italy but much less so here, and Dornfelder, a German red vinifera with an earthy nose and a Beaujolais-like taste. At present only Fulkerson and Red Tail Ridge offer a Dornfelder wine. Also in the cold-climate grape category is their Grüner Veltliner, another increasingly popular, but still scarce, variety in the Finger Lakes.

Fulkerson gets very busy in the fall, when area home winemakers descend to buy over thirty different varieties of fresh grape juice on which to try their own winemaking skills, and to stock up on home winemaking supplies.

Glenora Wine Cellars

Glenora is a well-established, well-respected winery whose roots run deeper than all but a handful of Finger Lakes producers. Co-owner Gene Pierce, one of the pioneers of the Finger Lakes wine industry, founded Glenora along with three other partners in 1978, just after passage of the Farm Winery Act in 1976 (see page 46). Today the many wineries on Seneca Lake seem to shoot by as one drives along Route 14 on the west or 414 on the east—yet Glenora was the very first.

Gene Pierce of Glenora Wine Cellars, the first winery on Seneca Lake.

Glenora Falls

Today Glenora is owned by Pierce and his business partner Scott Welliver, who also own Chateau LaFayette Reneau and Knapp Winery. Over the years Glenora has blossomed from a winery to a full destination spot, complete with a popular restaurant (called Veraisons) and lodging facility in addition to the tasting room. In the past *Wine Spectator* has named Glenora one of the top wineries in the world.

Glenora takes its name from nearby Glenora Road, which in turn is named for Glenora Falls, pictured on the bottle labels. (Head down either South or North Glenora Road and you should be able to get a glimpse of the falls, with the railroad trestle crossing above.)

Vineyards surrounding the winery provide grapes, along with some from Knapp and from other growers throughout the region, most from Seneca and Cayuga Lakes, some from Keuka. The winemaker here, as well as at Knapp, is Steve DiFrancesco, whose pedigree stretches back to the early days of quality wine in the Finger Lakes, having worked for Charles Fournier at Gold Seal in the late 1970s. DiFrancesco focuses on Riesling but at Glenora he produces a wide range of vinifera, hybrids, blends, and native-grape wines. Winemaking techniques of course vary with the grape and style of wine being produced. One departure from the norm here is the use of a concrete egg-shaped fermentation tank to make Pinot Blanc and some other whites. (The egg is on display at Knapp Winery and is discussed on page 93.) There are two egg-tanks here at Glenora, one at Knapp. The object of the egg, briefly put, is to impart some of the rounder mouthfeel that the winemaker gets with oak-barrel fermentation, without any of the oak taste.

Glenora offers a very instructive Stave and Steel Wine Tour of the winery from November through May, showcasing the various ways to make wine: stainless steel, oak barrels, the egg, and the complex champagne method (*méthode champenoise*) for sparkling wines.

Notable wines here include the Rieslings (Glenora had the first Riesling released on Seneca Lake, in 1978), and various white vinifera: Chardonnay; Pinot Blanc (often produced three ways—fermented in stainless steel, barrel-fermented, and egg-fermented); Signature, a nice and unusual blend of Pinot Blanc, Chardonnay, and Riesling; and a Gewurz. Dry hybrid whites include a Seyval Blanc. In reds they have the two Cabs, with Cab Franc done both oaked and stainless-steel-only, a rare (for the Finger Lakes) Sangiovese, Merlot, and Syrah. Glenora was an early producer of Syrah in the region, making this wine since 2006. A red blend called Yellow Cab mixes Cab Franc, Baco Noir, and a rarely seen Cornell hybrid called Geneva Red. Reds also include a Meritage in the classic Cab Sauv-Cab Franc-Merlot combination, and a blend called Black Diamond Express (a nod to the name of the train that once ran along the tracks below the winery), which mixes Cab Franc and Merlot with hybrids Baco Noir and Noiret. Sparklings include a vintage brut (a Chardonnay and Pinot Noir blend) when available, and a non-vintage sparkler. Dessert wines have port, ice wines (sometimes including a rare Cab Franc ice wine), and others.

Glenora is a large producer by Finger Lakes standards, at about 55,000 cases per year.

Hazlitt 1852 Vineyards

Hazlitt has a "problem," the sort of problem just about every Finger Lakes winery would like to have. For Hazlitt 1852 Vineyards is in many ways two very different wineries in one. On Seneca Lake's eastern shore is the main winery, with fifty acres of grapevines and a list of well-made vinifera and hybrid table wines. In Naples, New York, on Canandaigua Lake, is Hazlitt's Red Cat Cellars, a large winemaking facility capable of

Hazlitt 1852 Vineyards, on Seneca Lake.

Hazlitt's Red Cat Winery, formerly Widmer's, in Naples.

producing some three million gallons of wine—once the home of Widmer's, an early Finger Lakes winery that closed its doors in 2011—dedicated mostly, but not entirely, to making Hazlitt's Red Cat, a wildly popular Catawba wine that has an interesting history.

Introduced in the late 1970s, Red Cat began life as a homemade wine that owner Jerry Hazlitt made for himself and friends from the Catawba grapes (the "Cat" in Red Cat, although the wine also has some red hybrid wine blended in) grown on the property. Hazlitt was a grape grower, not a winemaker, and most of his grapes went to grape-products companies, like Welch's, which dominated the industry at the time. In the 1970s competition for these sales from California growers increased, and the grape-juice companies started to source outside the Finger Lakes. Hazlitt had a lot of Catawba they didn't know what to do with. Friends and neighbors suggested they make their homemade wine on a larger scale and see if it would sell.

Did it ever. Today Red Cat is the best-selling wine in New York State and accounts for about half the total dollar sales of Finger Lakes wine, at somewhere beyond 200,000 cases per year for Red Cat alone. Besides the wine you can buy Red Cat clothing and giftware. There's even a Red Cat mascot in a furry suit.

The other Hazlitt, much like many other high-quality wineries in the area, produces a range of excellent red and white vinifera and hybrid wines. The "1852" in Hazlitt 1852 refers to the year when family patriarch David Hazlitt purchased 153 acres of vineyard and orchards in Hector. The Hazlitt family has been here ever since, and the winery is now owned by the sixth generation. All their vinifera wines are estate-grown, with one exception. Their Schooner red and white blends are dry wines with Malbec from Argentina in the red, and Sauvignon Blanc from New Zealand in the white. (Co-owner Doug Hazlitt is a ship-restoration enthusiast, specializing in old schooners.) In both cases juice is imported and the wine made in the Hector winery. Their Gruvee is a *frizzante* (slightly effervescent) version of Grüner Veltliner. And they offer a port, some ice wines, and a very interesting solera sherry, made from native Concord and Elvira grapes and aged in true solera style in barrels placed on the roof of the Naples winery.

The signature snack in the tasting room is popcorn, in tribute to founder Jerry Hazlitt, who loved chatting with tasters and munching popcorn with them while sitting at the horseshoe-shaped tasting-room bar.

Hector Wine Company

This is a relatively new winery with some old and deep Finger Lakes roots. Owned by winemaker Justin Boyette (formerly at Atwater) and viticulturist Jason Hazlitt, whose family has been growing grapes in the region for well over a century, Hector sources its grapes from Sawmill Creek Vineyards, the renowned Banana Belt acreage that supplies many of the top wineries in the Finger Lakes. Hector's first vintage was in 2009 and the tasting room opened in 2010. Beams in the ceiling and planks that make up the tasting-room bar were repurposed from an old agricultural building on the site.

Hector features vinifera made with minimal intervention and native fermentation, using wild, indigenous yeasts, for most of the reds. Grapes are all handpicked and carefully sorted. Among the whites is a Pinot Blanc, a fairly unusual grape in the Finger Lakes, with a texture similar to fine Chardonnay. Like Chardonnay it undergoes a softening malolactic secondary fermentation and it ferments and ages in oak. The vines for this wine are ancient by Finger Lakes standards, planted in 1983. Their Riesling is a classic Finger Lakes expression, dry and minerally, fermented in stainless steel, and they have a Gewürztraminer and a Pinot Gris among the whites as well. Soul Red is their "everyday" red blend, mostly Chelois (an Albert Seibel hybrid, originating in France) plus Cabernet Franc, Cabernet Sauvignon, and Merlot. The complementary Soul White is semi-dry blend of hybrids Cayuga, Ravat, and Vidal Blanc. Hector also has the rare (for here) Syrah, the oldest Syrah grapes in the Finger Lakes, planted in 1998. A white and a blush wine made from native Catawba round out the menu.

Essence is their high-end red blend, with the Bordeaux-style recipe of Cabernet Sauvignon, Merlot, and Cabernet Franc, aged eleven months in oak. Fruit for this wine is selected from their best output of the three grape varieties. (Many American wine drinkers, accustomed to the "best" wine being a varietal like Chardonnay or Cabernet Sauvignon, assume blends are what winemakers do with leftover or second-rate grapes. This isn't the case. Remember, many of the world's acknowledged great wines, from Bordeaux to Riojas, Super Tuscans and beyond, are blends.)

Hector Wine Company produces in the area of 4,000 cases per year. Like others in this size, they are making outstanding wines with careful attention to getting the best out of first-rate grapes. A tasting-room visit will also introduce Forge Cellars, a separate winery with some overlap in ownership (Hector co-owner Boyette is also a partner in Forge).

Kemmeter Wines

Kemmeter is one of the youngest wineries in the Finger Lakes, yet one of the most interesting and promising at the same time. Kemmeter is the fulfillment of a dream of the co-owner and winemaker, Johannes Reinhardt, whose story is extensively chronicled in Evan Dawson's excellent book on the people at the forefront of Finger Lakes winemaking, *Summer in a Glass.* Reinhardt is a native of Germany, growing up in a family of farmers and winemakers whose history goes back far into the past: The family crest on the Kemmeter label (Kemmeter is his grandmother's maiden name) was bestowed on the family in 1438 by Emperor Albrecht II. Reinhardt received his formal training in vineyard management and winemaking in Germany and worked in wineries there for some years. In 1999 he arrived in the United States and spent one harvest at Dr. Konstantin Frank Vinifera Wine Cellars. The next year he became winemaker at Anthony Road Wine Company, which is directly across the road from the Kemmeter vineyard. In 2013 he and his wife, Imelda, opened the tasting room at Kemmeter Wines, surrounded by fields and now, by vineyards.

Reinhardt has about twenty acres surrounding the tasting-room building, of which six acres have yielded Kemmeter's first estate wines. Otherwise the Kemmeter wines are sourced from a vineyard near Rochester called White Pine Vineyard, as well as Sheldrake on Cayuga Lake and Red Tail Ridge a few miles north of Kemmeter. But Reinhardt's goal is to have exclusively estate wines if at all possible—the target

Kemmeter's deer fence was the first project for the vineyard.

is the 2018 vintage but, as Reinhardt is quick to emphasize, growing quality vinifera grapes is a very humbling experience. "You have to be in the vineyard every day," he says. Bad things can, and do, happen quickly as the grapes and vines grow. Rain, hail, insect infestations, and more are all part of the grape grower's possible challenges.

Vineyard management and growing the best possible fruit makes up the bedrock of Reinhardt's winemaking. He began with a simple remedy for deer predation, constructing a deer fence around the entire property. ("Deer love Gewurz, especially," he says.) He has a young vineyard of Riesling, Pinot Noir, and Pinot Blanc, and he'll soon be adding Gewurz and probably Zweigelt. Reinhardt contends that a well-established vineyard is not a prerequisite to yielding good grapes. What matters is the healthiness of the vines. If plants are healthy they survive the winters; extreme cold, for example, could wipe out 70 percent or more of an unhealthy vineyard, devastating the winery. Healthy vines would sustain far less loss. Toward this end he practices cluster-thinning, which rests the vine, and meticulous canopy management—the "canopy" being the grape leaves at the top of the vines. Half of disease control is good canopy management, as well as good siting that allows sunlight to dry the leaves as soon as possible in the morning. Even row direction can play a role. The first Kemmeter vineyard is planted diagonally, unusual for the area, and the reason was to strike a balance between sun exposure and airflow. In winter, as we have seen, vineyards routinely hill up the vines above the graft to protect the vine from cold, resulting in a series of long, low hills the length of each row. These hills will trap cold air in winter if they run perpendicular to the slope of the land. But a diagonal direction, pointing down the slope of the vineyard land toward the lake, allows this cold air to drain away and be replaced by warmer air later in the day.

These are but a few of the issues that the grape grower must contend with. Once the fruit is picked Reinhardt puts on his other hat, that of winemaker. (The actual winemaking is done, for now, across the road at Anthony Road.) He insists that winemaking is relatively uncomplicated compared with the challenges of growing great wine grapes. Less is definitely more in the winery. He manipulates the wines as little as possible, making winemaking a process of guiding the wine, rather than pushing it around. The winemaker, he says, should look to touch the wine as few times as possible. The goal is to bring out the quality inherent in the fruit. Toward this end Kemmeter does no fining, which can make a wine pleasant enough to drink right away, but tends to shorten the wine's life span dramatically.

As a result of these methods, he says, the Kemmeter wines will benefit from or even require more time in the bottle to showcase their best qualities. His first vintage release, in 2015, should stay in the bottle a year or two, even for the whites being produced (Riesling and a Pinot Noir–Pinot Gris blend called simply Pinot Cuvee). Reds—which are still to come as of this writing—will need three to five years in the bottle to reach their best.

Most lovers of Finger Lakes wines will find any Kemmeter product, even a right-away release, to be a memorable pour. Kemmeter produces wines under three labels: Sonero (a salsa-music lead singer gifted at improvisation) is the entry-level, less formal wine; Kemmeter, the main label for the winery; and SanSan (his wife Imelda's name in Chinese) is the reserve-wine label, produced only in select vintage years when the quality of the fruit is exceptional. For now, Riesling is the main focus of all labels, with the Pinot Cuvee as well. Other varieties will follow, including the Zweigelt, a red wine from Austria and a very common grape there, but very uncommon here. It tends to over-crop, meaning it produces lots of grapes, which is good if the goal is abundant grapes, not so good if the goal is grapes of the highest quality. Careful cluster-thinning results in a very different wine from the commodity red it produces in Austria. Zweigelt can show more tannin and boldness than its cousin Lemberger if handled correctly, and Reinhardt hopes he can produce a wine with real body and stamina.

Kemmeter production is small, just 400 cases as of now, with a goal of only 1500 cases. Reinhardt wants to remain small and, above all, hands-on in both the vineyard and the winery. Kemmeter Wines is open only by appointment—information for making one is on the Kemmeter website. Any serious wine lover with an interest in the best-quality Finger Lakes wine is well advised to book that appointment.

King's Garden Vineyards

Owner, winemaker, and vineyardist Mike Oleksyn planted his first vines for King's Garden in 1998. Today the vineyard consists of sixteen acres planted at Lodi Point, across Route 414 and down toward Seneca Lake in the Banana Belt. The name King's Garden is a reference to the vineyards maintained by troops garrisoned in the Thousand Islands during the French and Indian Wars; they called their vineyards King's Garden. Of the sixteen acres, five are devoted to Chardonnay and virtually all the rest to vinifera reds: the two Cabs, Merlot, Pinot Noir, and Syrah.

At King's Garden all the vinifera wines are estate wines. The emphasis here is on reds, especially "big, bold reds," many of which are aged three years or more in the barrel. Reds include Pinot Noir, Cabernet Franc, Merlot, Syrah, a Meritage called Knights Blend, and their signature King's Cab, a 100 percent Cabernet Sauvignon that also has a reserve bottling. White vinifera on offer is Chardonnay only, presented in different vintages with the whole spectrum of barrel versus stainless-steel fermentation—some wines fully oaked, some not at all, others somewhere in between.

King's Garden produces a rare late-harvest Chardonnay for a dessert wine. Other sweeter wines include blends and hybrids with medieval-inspired names like Wicked Wench.

They produce something over 2,000 cases per year at the winery, which is up the hill east of the tasting room.

Lakewood Vineyards

Lakewood's beginnings under ownership by the Stamp family stretch back to the very early days of modern Finger Lakes winemaking, when in 1951 then-dentist Frank Stamp decided to take up farming in upstate New York. He bought a run-down orchard just north of Watkins Glen and began planting labrusca and hybrid grapes to sell to the local wineries and juice companies. Lakewood kept up commercial grape growing until 1988, when Frank's son Monty Stamp began making wine from the grapes grown in their vineyard. (Monty, who died in 2007, was a revered figure in Finger Lakes winemaking, one of the founding members of the New York State Wine Grape Growers, an important trade organization.) Lakewood's wines have continued ever since, still with the extended Stamp family at the helm.

The Lakewood vineyard supplies about 80 percent of the grapes for Lakewood wines, the remainder coming from nearby vineyards. They produce a relatively extensive array of vinifera, hybrid, and labrusca wines that are successfully food-friendly and satisfying. Lakewood cultivates about eighty acres of vines and at this writing is planting another recently purchased hundred acres. They are also expanding their production facility to add tanks and make the tank and barrel rooms more accessible to visitors. Their central building, with a south-facing roof, boasts an impressive solar-panel array that produces 80 percent of their electric needs for the actual wine-producing part of the winery, which requires the most energy.

Lakewood produces about 10,000 cases per year of their Lakewood-label wines, with about another 20,000 cases produced for other wineries. Despite this relatively high production level the Lakewood wines show considerable attention to craft and have won numerous awards. Winemaker Chris Stamp (Monty's son) grew up on the Lakewood farm so he knows his grapes, some of which he tended while working on the farm. His brother Dave Stamp is the vineyard manager and a well-known vineyardist in the region.

Lakewood produces excellent examples of many of the usual suspects in Finger Lakes wines, from Rieslings to Chardonnay, Gewurz, and Vignoles, plus Pinot Noir, Cab Franc, and Lemberger. One unusual offering is a mead, a wine made from honey, called Seifu's Tej. This mead is made in the Ethiopian style (tej), which is a little spicier than most meads, this one made to order for a small chain of Ethiopian restaurants in the Detroit area. (The honey comes from nearby Wixson's Honey.) At times they have sparkling *méthode champenoise* wines and offer a carbonated Catawba-based sweet wine called Candeo. Lakewood also makes a Valvin Muscat, a fruity, semi-sweet Cornell hybrid first released in 2006, and an iced wine, called Glaciovinum, made from the native Delaware grape.

The rose on the Lakewood labels showcases a long-standing tradition of growing roses at Lakewood, which dates back to the pre-winery days of the Lakewood Farm. Today the winery is surrounded by several hundred rosebushes, which make for an impressive display beginning with the June bloom.

Lamoreaux Landing Wine Cellars

Lamoreaux Landing consistently produces outstanding vinifera wines from grapes grown exclusively in their own vineyards. Owner Mark Wagner planted the first vines in the early 1970s, and released his first wines in 1992. (Wagner is a distant cousin to the Wagners of Wagner Vineyard, just south of Lamoreaux Landing, both planting vines on land owned by prior generations of Wagners, but other than the name and a family connection reaching back several generations, there is no connection between the two wineries.) Lamoreaux Landing, whose name derives from a nineteenth-century steamboat landing on the shore of Seneca Lake just west of the winery, is housed in an airy, spacious,

and dramatic building with a tasting room on the entry floor and the winery operation in the basement below. Affording one of the finest views of fields, vineyards, and Seneca Lake stretching northward, the Lamoreaux Landing tasting room is a delightful space.

Made all the more delightful by the wines, which rank among the very best the Finger Lakes has to offer. *Wine & Spirits* magazine named LL one of the top one hundred wineries in the world, twice in three years (2010 and 2012). Lamoreaux vineyards include those immediately surrounding the winery, but also many plots along Route 414 to the south. The vineyards have homespun names: Red Oak Vineyard has a red oak tree, Black Diamond Vineyard is crossed by the old railroad line that ran the Black Diamond train, and Yellow Dog Vineyard is the namesake of Wagner's yellow Lab (named Max); the name of SVAT Vineyard stands for "Seyval and Vidal Above the Tracks" (another reference to the railroad), which quizzically enough hosts only Vidal (for ice wine), the Seyval having given way to plantings of Pinot Noir, Merlot, and Gewürztraminer. The Ives Vineyard is named for a labrusca variety planted in the 1960s, which was later field-grafted (in other words, the grafting is done in situ rather than in a nursery) with Chardonnay onto the Ives roots. These are Lamoreaux's oldest vines and this remains one of very, very few field-grafted vineyards in the Finger Lakes.

Although Lamoreaux produces an extensive and adventurous variety of vinifera—about which more below—the winery is perhaps best known for its Riesling. Lamoreaux offers Riesling in many guises, from dry to sweet. Tasters can sample single-vineyard Rieslings, which indeed display different flavor notes as an expression of the differences in the soils in which the vines grow (known as terroir). Many of the LL Rieslings are attractively priced for their quality.

In all Lamoreaux Landing offers the following: Riesling, Chardonnay, Gewürztraminer, Muscat Ottonel, and Grüner Veltliner among the vinifera whites, and Cabernet Franc, Cabernet Sauvignon, Pinot Noir, and Merlot in reds. Their lone hybrid offering is a Vidal ice wine, and they produce two sparkling whites from Chardonnay, a brut and a blanc de blancs. Intriguing among these is the Grüner Veltliner, a popular cool-climate variety in Europe but not extensively planted in the Finger Lakes. Lamoreaux's GV got its genesis in a trip Mark Wagner took to Austria in the company of acclaimed chef and restaurateur Dano Hudnik, proprietor of Dano's Heuriger just north of the winery. Hudnik pointed Wagner toward the Austrian Grüner Veltliner, a fruity, complex wine that trends somewhere between dry Riesling and Gewürztraminer, and Wagner decided to give it a try in the Finger Lakes. Although more cold-sensitive than Riesling, the Lamoreaux Grüner Veltliner has weathered the winters so far (even the intensely cold winters of 2013–14 and 2014–15) and makes an impressive wine. Another interesting experiment is found among the reds, with the T23 Cab Franc. This is a completely un-oaked wine, virtually unheard of for Cabernet Franc, and makes a delightfully crisp, intensely flavored wine. The T23 designation, by the way, comes from the tank that first held the wine, Tank #23.

As one may gather from the Grüner Veltliner and the T23 Cab Franc, Wagner and his winemaker at Lamoreaux, Colin Grant, are adventurous crafters of excellent wine, interested in expanding the horizon for what can be made in the Finger Lakes. Case quantity here is about 12,000 to 15,000 cases annually.

Leidenfrost Vineyards

This is a slightly ironic name for a vineyard right in the warm Banana Belt of southeastern Seneca Lake, because it means "suffer the cold" in German. The vines here probably do suffer, if a plant can suffer, but they don't quit, making for one of the oldest and best vineyard sites in the Finger Lakes.

Leidenfrost (it's pronounced *LYE-den-frost*, not *LEE-den-frost*) began in 1942 when John Leidenfrost Sr. bought a farm planted with Concord grapes and fruit trees. Over the next several years he planted more grapes, mostly Catawba, and by the 1950s was a steady supplier of Catawba to Gold Seal. He added hybrids, including Cayuga and Baco Noir vines that are still in cultivation, but most of the vineyard activity

went into growing and selling Catawba to Gold Seal and, later, Great Western.

In 1984 his son John Leidenfrost Jr., the current owner, took over management of the vineyard. By then the market for labrusca grapes like Catawba was in decline. One day he was on his sailboat on Seneca Lake looking at the vineyard land, thinking that the grapes there had no future, when the answer came to him: Plant vinifera.

It was mostly a business decision. Vinifera got five times the price of Catawba ($1,500 per ton vs $300 per ton). He had seen his neighbor, Hazlitt's Sawmill Creek Vineyard, turn to vinifera five years earlier and find success with it. So he began pulling up Catawba and planting Merlot, Chardonnay, Pinot Noir, and more. Most of the current vineyard was planted in the period from 1984 to 1992.

Until 1990 Leidenfrost was a vineyard only, selling grapes to area wineries. The vineyard site is remarkable; despite brutally cold winters they have never been frozen out, never lost a vine to cold that did not come back eventually. Likewise in the spring frosts they have never lost a crop to freezing. There is a seven-degree temperature difference between the vineyard close to the lake and the top of the hill. The vineyards extend to about a thousand feet short of the lakeshore.

Leidenfrost has twenty-eight acres planted here and another ten acres slightly to the north in Valois.

Leidenfrost decided early on that he would plant vinifera grapes for wines he liked himself—the reds, including Pinot Noir and the Cabernets. They continue to be prime varietals at Leidenfrost, with the Pinot Noir including a clone, arriving here under murky circumstances, from the famed Burgundy vineyard Clos de Vougeot. (It's worth noting that Clos de Vougeot was a mature vineyard by the year 1336, a fact that helps highlight the head start that European winemakers have over their colleagues in the Finger Lakes.)

Leidenfrost had been a home winemaker throughout the 1980s and in 1990 produced his first commercial Leidenfrost Vineyards wine. For the first few years of the 1990s the tasting room was in the log cabin close to the road, near the current tasting room and winery building, which was constructed in 1996. Today about half of the vineyard's fruit goes to Leidenfrost wine, the rest being sold to distinguished area wineries: Dr. Frank, Billsboro, Damiani, Hector Wine Co., and others.

Today John Leidenfrost is joined by daughter Liz Leidenfrost, who serves as assistant winemaker, tasting-room manager, and often vineyard associate as well. The Leidenfrosts' winemaking is traditional in orientation. Reds are aged in the barrel for two to three years. Whites are all stainless-steel-fermented (Chardonnay excepted), not oaked.

Leidenfrost produces about twenty different varieties of wine. In the reds they offer Merlot, Baco Noir, the two Cabs, Pinot Noir, a Meritage blend (Rhapsody), and two other blends, one semi-dry (Burlesque) and one dry (Tango, a Pinot Noir–Baco Noir combination). Whites include Chardonnay, Riesling, Gewürztraminer, Cayuga, and a new offering, Grüner Veltliner. White blends include Sonata, combining Cayuga White with Vignoles, and various semi-sweet Catawba-based blends. In sparkling they offer a traditional blanc-de-blancs produced *méthode champenoise* and a carbonated Cayuga White. Dessert wines include a pair of ports, one white and one red.

Leidenfrost is a small winery (about 3,000 cases per year), all estate-grown from some of the best vineyard land in the Finger Lakes. Leidenfrost lets the grapes speak for themselves, producing first-rate wines that anyone, and especially red-wine fans, will enjoy.

Penguin Bay Winery

This is the third winery owned by the Peterson family, along with Swedish Hill and Goose Watch. Penguin Bay opened in 2005, in what was formerly the Finger Lakes Champagne House. The name Penguin Bay is a nod to the Peterson's generosity toward the Rosamond Gifford Zoo in Syracuse, specifically the Humboldt Penguins Exhibit, which receives a portion of the Penguin Bay annual proceeds as a donation. Fruit is sourced from Swedish Hill, and the winemaking is done there as well.

Notable wines here include New York State's first Moscato, made from Valvin Muscat, and an interesting red blend called Humboldt Red, which tastes very much like Shiraz but is made from two recent Cornell-developed hybrids, Corot Noir and Noiret, with a bit of vinifera Cab Sauvignon and Merlot. Other wines include a range of red and white vinifera and hybrids, and blends.

Prejean Winery

Pronounce this one right and you'll make owner Tom Prejean happy, because few people outside the area manage it: It's originally a French name, and pronounced *pray-JAWN.* But don't worry, a mispronunciation won't get you any less of a welcome at the winery.

Prejean started, like so many other area wineries, with the dream of a couple, in this case Jim and Elizabeth Prejean, to get out of the rush of "normal" life and enjoy owning a winery. The Prejeans were living in

Connecticut in the mid-1970s and bought fifty-three acres on the west side of Seneca Lake in 1979. They planted grapes and were tending the vineyard on weekends while still living in Connecticut until coming up full-time in 1985, when the winery was built. The first vintage was in 1986. Jim Prejean died suddenly in 1989, only three years after that first vintage, sadly missing the future growth of the winery that was to come. Jim and Elizabeth's son, Tom Prejean, the current owner, stepped in soon thereafter and has been running the winery ever since.

Prejean has about thirty acres of grapes in cultivation, growing Merlot (this is one of the earliest Merlot plantings in the Finger Lakes), Cabernet Sauvignon, Cabernet Franc, Riesling, Gewürztraminer, Chardonnay, and Pinot Noir as well as hybrids Marechal Foch, Noiret, Cayuga White, and others. Wines are all estate wines, made from grapes grown on the property, and include varietals of all of the vinifera grown and a few blends. Proprietor's Red (Foch and Noiret) is dry, others semi-sweet to sweet: Red and White Lotus, Cabana Frank, and Tiger Lily. Prejean also offers a relatively rare Marechal Foch varietal that is a nice example of a wine that isn't often able to stand on its own. Also rare (and good) is their Moscato. Their Goldfinch Vineyards label is a reserve wine, for Chardonnay and Riesling bottlings.

The winemaker here is Jim Zimar, who has been on board since the very beginning. Prejean produces about 4,000 cases per year and sells fruit to other wineries as well.

Ravines Wine Cellars

Ravines Wine Cellars was opened by owners Morten Hallgren, a French winemaker, and his wife, Lisa, a chef and his partner in the business, on seventeen acres on Keuka Lake in 2000. The ravines of Ravines are to be found there, although the winery today is located on Seneca Lake, just south of Geneva, nestled into the Silver Springs Vineyard. The Keuka Lake location remains as a satellite tasting room, although all of the estate vineyards and winemaking happen at the Seneca Lake location.

Hallgren comes from a very long tradition in winemaking—his family's vineyards in Provence, called Domaine de Castel Roubine, date back to the fourteenth century. Trained in both winemaking and viticulture in Montepellier, France, Hallgren began his career in wine at the famed Bordeaux estate Château Cos d'Estournel. After coming to the United States he was offered the post of head winemaker at Dr. Konstantin Frank Vinifera Wine Cellars, which he held for six years until, in 2000, the Hallgrens purchased the acreage on Keuka Lake and set to build Ravines. They opened the Keuka Lake tasting room in 2003.

Hallgren's first vintage was the 2002, made at rented space at the nearby Crooked Lake Winery. Later wines were made at Shaw, again with rented production space, and eventually at White Springs Winery, the former name for the current winery and vineyard on Seneca Lake. In 2012 the Hallgrens purchased the White Springs Winery from Carl Fribolin and renamed it Ravines. The quality of the vineyard, one of the few limestone soil vineyards in the Finger Lakes, as well as the sophisticated and capacious production facility, led the Hallgrens to make the purchase.

Ravines presents an excellent assortment of dry and semi-dry wines, mostly vinifera, but their signature wine is dry Riesling. About 40 percent of their production is Riesling, with Cabernet Franc a close second. The winery, housed in a former dairy barn, follows the familiar old-barn pattern of tasting room above, winery and barrel room below. Follow the instructions on the Ravines website if you choose to visit, and avoid White Springs Road. The winery is on Barracks Road in Geneva; don't try to access from the east, from White Springs Road, as this section of Barracks Road (1) is unpaved; (2) has signage telling you not to do it; and (3) is blocked by a padlocked gate just before you reach the winery, and you'll have to turn around. Take the next road to the west, the intriguingly named Pre-emption Road (aka County Road 6), and turn onto Barracks Road from there. The orchard you pass through on the way down the hill, flanking the vineyard, hosts trees belonging to the well-known local fruit farm Red Jacket Orchards.

Most of Ravines wines come from the White Springs Vineyard surrounding the winery. The White Springs themselves are key to the vineyard's success, as they irrigate the site naturally, making it one of the few vineyards in the region with such a feature. Other fruit is sourced from the Argetsinger Vineyard, on the other side of Seneca Lake, which is the source for a mineral-rich, single-vineyard dry Riesling, and the 16 Falls Vineyard in Lodi. The latter is on a long-term lease with the Hallgrens and is slated to be added to their vineyard holdings.

Ravines produces a relatively modest menu of wines, but what they offer is of outstanding quality. In addition to the Rieslings and Cabernet Franc, they produce Pinot Noir, Gewürztraminer, and Chardonnay varietals, a Meritage (Bordeaux-style) blend, and another red blend, Cerise, which combines Pinot Noir and Lemberger. Their informal Keuka Village white and red, the names harking back to the original Keuka Lake location, are blends of Cayuga and Vignoles, and Noiret and Cabernet Franc. The very appealing, fruity Ayre is a semi-dry Valvin Muscat with just a bit of fizz, and when conditions in the vineyard allow it they offer some *méthode champenoise* sparkling wines and late-harvest dessert wines.

Case quantity at Ravines is about 20,000 per year.

Red Newt Cellars

Red Newt got its start in 1998 when David and Debra Whiting decided to open both a winery and a restaurant simultaneously. David was the winemaker: He had learned the craft while working at McGregor, Chateau LaFayette Reneau, Swedish Hill, and Standing Stone. Debra was the chef: Although a Cornell microbiologist, her passion was food and how it could be best expressed through local Finger Lakes sourcing. Red Newt Bistro opened in 1999, coincident with the release of the first Red Newt wines.

Why the name? The Whitings lived on rural acreage with a pond, just north of the winery. Near the pond a common little critter was the eastern red spotted newt. Already the Whitings' focus was a celebration of things local—in food and wine—and they wanted a "local" name for their new winery. Hence Red Newt. The name is echoed in names of selected wines, like Viridescens and Notopthalmus—the scientific name for the red spotted newt is *Notophthalmus viridescens*. And a Hellbender (one of their port-style wines) is a species of giant salamander that lives in the Finger Lakes region.

Sadly the Finger Lakes lost one of its brightest stars in 2011 when Debra Whiting was killed in an auto accident, well known and much admired as a leader of the Finger Lakes locavore movement. The bistro she created continues and is a favored destination for excellent dining and outstanding views.

Red Newt is among the top producers of quality Finger Lakes wine. Their wine list is not extensive but what they do, they do very well. Virtually all Red Newt wines are vinifera, and the major focus at Red Newt is dry and semi-dry wines. Riesling is a specialty, from their entry-level Circle Riesling to a number of single-vineyard offerings from dry to sweet. Other whites at Red Newt include Pinot Gris and Gewürztraminer. Reds are represented by Cabernet Franc, Cabernet Sauvignon, and Merlot. (Red Newt has also produced Pinot Noir in the past and of course may do so again when the winemakers are so inclined.)

While the focus here is dry and semi-dry wines, an exception is what they call the Essences, dessert wines that are not really wines but slightly fermented vinifera grape juices to which are added grape-based spirits. Although not high in alcohol by comparison with liqueurs, at 14 to 16 percent alcohol, the spirits do come through and result in a refreshing after-dinner glass. Other dessert wine includes the port-style Hellbender.

Although the winery is surrounded by grapevines, all fruit for Red Newt wines is sourced from other vineyards. All are Finger Lakes, of course, and most are a stone's throw away, including Sawmill Creek,

Tango Oaks, and others. The winemaking reins have been passed from Whiting to Kelby James Russell, one of the new generation of Finger Lakes winemakers who are exploring the region's expanding opportunities and tend to focus on single-vineyard, terroir-based wines with relatively little intervention. Russell worked at Fox Run and at wineries in New Zealand and Australia before becoming winemaker at Red Newt.

Red Newt is among the more experimental and adventurous of Finger Lakes wineries. One such experiment, which points to the closeness of the Finger Lakes winemaking community, is the Tierce label. Begun in 2006 with wines from the 2004 vintage, Tierce is a collaboration among Red Newt, Fox Run, and Anthony Road first proposed by Johannes Reinhardt when he was winemaker at Anthony Road. The wineries bring wines from the same vintage year—usually Riesling, although they've also tried reds—and blend them together until they agree they have a wine that excels. The wines have produced extremely satisfactory results: The 2010 Tierce Dry Riesling, for example, was served at the presidential inauguration lunch in January 2013 to accompany lobster with clam-chowder sauce.

Red Newt produces approximately 20,000 cases per year, putting it at the upper end of Finger Lakes producers of quality table wine.

As you leave Red Newt's Tichenor Road and head south, you'll cross over Sawmill Creek, which gives its name to one of the prominent vineyards in the area (and a source for many grapes vinified at Red Newt). Sawmill Creek Vineyards is just across Route 414 after leaving Red Newt.

Red Tail Ridge Winery

A lot of interesting and unusual things are happening at Red Tail Ridge, detailed below, but let's begin with the founders, the husband-and-wife team of Mike Schnelle and Nancy Irelan, who arrived on the western shore of Seneca Lake in 2004. Prior to this they were involved in business and finance, with practical experience in construction (Mike) and industrial/corporate winemaking at E & J Gallo in California (Nancy). These backgrounds have served them very well as they have built up Red Tail Ridge Winery and its excellent wines.

The winery sits on a thirty-five-acre property, surrounded by about twenty-one acres currently planted in vines. Of these, fourteen acres are Riesling, and the wine production focuses mostly on Riesling, Chardonnay, and Pinot Noir. Mike Schnelle handles the vineyard and Nancy Irelan is the winemaker, although both are involved in the many other aspects of running a winery. The winery namesake is a pair of red-tailed hawks who nest in the woods to the right as you approach the winery.

Red Tail Ridge is not quite an estate-only winery, although that is the long-term goal. Any fruit that is sourced from other growers comes exclusively from Seneca Lake. The wines are produced mostly in small lots with a definite emphasis on quality over quantity. Red Tail produces excellent examples of many of the wines one might expect at a quality Finger Lakes winery: Chardonnay, both oaked and un-oaked, Riesling in various levels of residual sugar, a Gewurz, a Pinot Noir, and a Blaufränkisch (aka Lemberger). Beyond the high quality of the wines what sets Red Tail apart are the many intriguing experiments they sometimes offer as well. A *pétillant naturel* Riesling is one example, which involves wild-yeast fermentation and minimal intervention and yields a wine that is slightly fizzy *(pétillant)* and which by design varies widely from bottle to bottle. Another would be their wine called Miscreant, an "orange" or more accurately "ambered" wine, a blend of Chardonnay and Pinot Gris that is left on extended (fifteen days) skins contact and then barrel-aged for sixteen months. Perhaps most unusual is an ongoing series of experiments in relatively obscure red-wine varietals. These include Teroldego (*terr-ALL-de-go*), a grape from northern Italy that produces a fruity, spicy aromatic red a bit like Syrah. They are the only Finger Lakes producers currently growing Teroldego, and only one other winery in New York State, Channing Daughters on Long Island, produces a varietal. Also in the obscure-red program is Dornfelder, rarely seen here (Fulkerson also offers it), a German red-wine grape, and one more still in the vineyard, Lagrein, also a red from northern Italy. Red Tail promises more surprises in the obscure-red program, which is welcome news for the Finger Lakes red-wine enthusiast. The program also highlights the dynamic nature of a relatively young wine-growing region such as the Finger Lakes, where there are still many varieties that have never been attempted before.

Of special interest is the Red Tail winery building itself, so very different from the old-barn look that characterizes many Finger Lakes wineries. Opened in the fall of 2009, the large box-like metal building is the first LEED Gold-certified "green" winery building in the Finger Lakes. (That's Leadership in Energy and Environmental Design certification from the United States Green Building Council.) Among its "green" features are the east-facing wall of windows, which allows so much light that they rarely need to put on lights at all in the daytime, and a geothermal heating and cooling system. This system involves piped glycol that runs throughout the building, which can be laptop-controlled to vary the temperature as needed in different areas of the winery. The temperature can be fifty-eight degrees Fahrenheit in the tank room and seventy degrees in the barrel-fermenting room, all while the usual twenty degrees of February takes hold outside. The entire wine-production process occurs here: pressing, tank room, barrel room, and bottling line. Still to come at Red Tail Ridge is equipment (currently on order) for producing *méthode champenoise* sparkling wines.

The "green" winery at Red Tail Ridge

Case quantity at Red Tail Ridge is about 8,000. This is a particularly dynamic and interesting winery that continues to surprise with excellent handcrafted wines and many wines found almost nowhere else.

Shalestone Vineyards

"I would never have this business if I didn't have the vineyard." So said co-owner Rob Thomas in a recent conversation in the tasting room at Shalestone Vineyards, which he and his wife, Kate Thomas, founded in 1998. Their six-and-a-half-acre vineyard on the eastern shore of Seneca Lake is on rocky, clay-rich terrain ideally suited to Shalestone's signature wines. "Red is all we do" is the motto here, and unlike any other Finger Lakes winery Shalestone produces red and red alone. The reasons are as multifaceted and layered as a good red wine. There is differentiation, of course, which provides Shalestone a unique identity. But the yearning to work on red wine is more personal. Reds suit Thomas's palate, he says, and he feels red wine provides a broader canvas for the winemaker's art.

Most red-wine lovers agree that Shalestone is succeeding superbly. Indeed, this winery is a must-visit for even the moderately serious red-wine enthusiast. The tasting room is small—no busloads here—and the servers, sometimes Rob Thomas himself, are eager to engage customers in talk of wine, the Finger Lakes, and anything else. Ironically the vineyards surrounding the Shalestone tasting room and production buildings (the latter built into the earth to keep temperatures steady and cool) are all Riesling grapes and belong to other wineries. The Shalestone vines are to the west, beyond the trees, closer to the shores of Seneca Lake.

Rob and Kate Thomas came to the Finger Lakes in the late 1970s, and Rob has been making wine in the area since 1986. They designed and built their winery in 1998, using cedar trees and hardwoods cleared from the vineyard below as material.

Shalestone grows Cabernet Sauvignon, Merlot, Cabernet Franc, Syrah, Lemberger, and Pinot Noir in their vineyard, and buys grapes from other local producers when its own production is insufficient. They produce varietals of all of the above except the Lemberger, which arrives as the driving force of a blend (with Syrah) called Lemberghini. Other blends include Synergy, Harmony, and Red Legend, all outstanding dry reds. Their sole departure from the red-only motto is a blend of Zweigelt (a cold-climate red-wine grape grown extensively in Austria) and Lemberger, vinified as a robustrosé and called Beyond Rosé.

Case quantity here is about 1,500 cases per year. Personal and singular, Shalestone's wines are an essential addition to the Finger Lakes wine rack.

Shaw Vineyard

Shaw ranks among the very best of the smaller producers in the Finger Lakes, and one of the most interesting and inventive. Winemaker and owner Steve Shaw, who began as a grape grower in the 1980s, became a winemaker in the '90s, and opened his winery and tasting room in 2004, has been described by *Wine Enthusiast*'s Anna Lee Iijima as "a bit of a mad scientist among top Finger Lakes producers"—a comment proudly displayed on a banner at the door of the tasting room. It's fair to say that Shaw experiments with winemaking methods more than with offbeat grape varieties or blends. His grape varieties, strictly vinifera for his wines, are grown on two Shaw vineyards, one on Seneca Lake sloping east toward the lake from the tasting room, and an older (planted 1980–81) vineyard on the east shore of Keuka Lake. The grapes, as noted, are what one would expect, but an abundant variety given that Shaw plants only about sixteen acres of vinifera: Riesling, Sauvignon Blanc, Gewürztraminer, Pinot Grigio, and Chardonnay in the whites, and Pinot Noir, Cabernet Franc, Cabernet Sauvignon, and Merlot in the reds.

It's in the winemaking that Shaw's "mad scientist" comes out. He waits on his grapes longer than most other growers, harvesting from mid-October to mid-November. This takes intestinal fortitude given Finger Lakes weather patterns, when hard freezes and snow in these weeks are always among Nature's options. But waiting allows Shaw grapes to be at their peak of flavor and sugars. And if the weather does turn against him Shaw still has considerable work to do: Every vinifera is hand-harvested. His next innovation is a crusher-destemmer that only destems, allowing him to treat red wines with ultimate TLC. Red-wine grapes get more of a massage than a crush—the juice runs out slowly, pressed by the weight of the berries themselves and stirred periodically by Shaw with a large wooden paddle. Whites, which need to get off the skins in most cases, are pressed with very low pressure to release the juice.

Shaw ages all reds in oak for at least eighteen months and often considerably longer, up to four years in some cases. (An exception that proves the rule here would be their un-oaked Cab Franc.) The barrel room is belowground, under the tasting room. Whites are oaked when appropriate, such as with Chardonnay. But in all cases Shaw's goal is to produce crisp, cool-climate, European-style wines the very best he can.

One recent experiment, tried by a few other Finger Lakes producers as well, is an "orange" wine, a style originally from the Caucasus that is enjoying a bit of a resurgence among adventurous winemakers. In simple terms orange wine is a white wine made as if it were a red—that is, the juice from a traditionally white-wine grape is left in contact with the skins for an extended period of time. The result is wine somewhere between a red and a white in taste and character, often with a distinctive orange hue. Shaw has a least a couple of orange wines, one from a blend of Sauvignon Blanc and Gewurz, the other a Gewurz varietal that has received high praise in the wine publications.

At something between 1,500 and 2,000 cases produced per year, Shaw emphasizes quality over quantity. As a result the wines are not the easiest to find in the average wine shop, even in the Finger Lakes. But they are well worth hunting down, and the tasting room is always well stocked.

Silver Thread Vineyard

Silver Thread Vineyard began life in 1982 when Richard Figiel, a local organics enthusiast (and author of the excellent book *Circle of Vines,* on the history of New York winemaking), set up a vineyard on six acres of prime Banana Belt Seneca Lake land. Dedicated to sustainable vineyard management from the start, and for a period in the 1990s a certified

organic winery, Silver Thread is home to carefully managed vineyards and very well-crafted wines, produced with care in relatively limited quantities. The first vintage was in 1991 and in 1995 Figiel constructed the current tasting room, which combines contemporary architectural lines with the classic Greek Revival style of the early-nineteenth-century farmhouses sprinkled throughout the Finger Lakes. Figiel sold the winery in 2011 to current owners Paul and Shannon Brock, who have continued and expanded the Silver Thread vision.

The winery gets its name from a nearby waterfall, Silver Thread Falls, and its stone-turtle logo is a reproduction of an ancient Iroquois stone carving, a tribute to the original Native American stewards of the land. The Iroquois had peach orchards on this stretch of Seneca slope some 250 years ago, taking early advantage of the lake-effect warmth that sustains the grapevines today.

The Brocks have an impressive Finger Lakes wine pedigree: Paul was the winemaker at Lamoreaux Landing before purchasing Silver Thread, and before that worked at Ravines and Keuka Lake Vineyards as well as a stint winemaking in New Zealand. Shannon is a certified wine judge and former wine director at the New York Wine & Culinary Center in Canandaigua.

The vineyards now comprise eight acres from the original six, all near the winery and tasting-room building. (The large vineyard you pass coming down Caywood Road is the Doyle family's large Chardonnay vineyard.) Sustainability remains a priority here, as it was for Richard Figiel—the Brocks have recently (2015) installed a solar-panel system that supplies all of the electricity needs for the winery and tasting room.

The showcase wine here is Riesling, but Silver Thread also offers Chardonnay, Gewurz, Pinot Noir, Cab Franc, and Cab Sauv, and there is a bit of Merlot in the vineyard for a future vintage. Virtually all the wines are dry, with a couple in a semi-dry style—no nods to the sweet-wine drinkers here. Many, but not all, wines are estate-grown—with eight acres some sourcing of outside fruit is not surprising.

The Riesling is produced in a dry and semi-dry style from their own STV Vineyard, and they have four single-vineyard Rieslings, all in a medium-dry style. First are those from the homegrown STV Vineyard as well as the neighboring vineyard, known as the Doyle Fournier Vineyard because the wines were planted in 1973 by the legendary Charles Fournier of Gold Seal. These are among the oldest vinifera plantings on Seneca Lake. From Keuka Lake comes the Gridley Bluff Point Vineyard Riesling, from a modest half acre on Keuka planted around 2008. The Randolph O'Neill Vineyard Riesling comes from Cayuga Lake.

Other whites are an estate-grown barrel-fermented Chardonnay, from Silver Thread's oldest vines, and a Gewürztraminer, also estate-grown.

Red varietals include an estate Pinot Noir, from vines planted in the mid-1990s, as well as Cabernet Sauvignon and Cabernet Franc. Two popular offerings are blends. Their red Blackbird, a wine named and originally produced by Richard Figiel, is a blend of mostly Cabernet Franc with additions of Merlot and Cabernet Sauvignon. The white blend is called Good Earth White and combines hybrid Vidal Blanc with some Riesling and Gewürztraminer.

Another recent offering is a dry rosé of Pinot Noir, adding another candidate to the selections of excellent Finger Lakes rosés produced throughout the region.

Silver Thread produces about 3,000 cases per year and would be an essential stop for the committed wine enthusiast.

Standing Stone Vineyards

Standing Stone Vineyards, on Seneca Lake's eastern shore, produces very high-quality whites and reds in one of the friendliest atmospheres around—in a wine region that is already noteworthy for the friendly accessibility of its owners and the staff who run the wineries and tasting rooms. Owners Tom and Marti Macinski bought their vineyards in 1991 from Gold Seal, the "legacy" winemaker famous for its very

early (for the Finger Lakes) experiments with vinifera grapes. Gold Seal president Charles Fournier, along with famed French winemaker Guy DeVeaux, first planted wine grapes on what is now Standing Stone Vineyards in the early 1970s, after an intensive analysis of locations that would be best for vinifera wine grapes. The result, after years of work on the part of the Macinskis, is an outstanding winery that must be on every Finger Lakes visitor's itinerary.

Standing Stone (the name refers to the shale that underlies virtually all the land in the Finger Lakes) focuses on wines that it does best, with forty-one acres surrounding the winery planted with Riesling, Gewürztraminer, Chardonnay, and Vidal on the white side, and for reds Cabernet Sauvignon, Petit Verdot (a vinifera grape traditionally, but today infrequently, used in Bordeaux), and Saperavi, another relatively obscure vinifera red, planted here in 1995 and also grown by Dr. Frank and McGregor Vineyard in the Finger Lakes. Both reds and whites are exceptional and unusual, the Saperavi—a red hailing originally from the republic of Georgia in Eastern Europe—yielding a very rich, complex, tannic wine that lovers of red must try. Another popular red at Standing Stone is their Smokehouse red blend, a combination of Cabernet Sauvignon, Saperavi, and Petit Verdot, sometimes from different vintage years, and aged eighteen to twenty-four months in American oak.

Standing Stone tends more to the dry-wine camp but offers some excellent sweet dessert wines, including an unusual Chardonnay ice wine as well as "ices" from Gewurz, Vidal, and Riesling. These ice wines are made from grapes picked very late in the year, after the leaves have dropped, and frozen after picking.

Standing Stone benefits from outstanding soil and, for many of their wines, from vines planted by Fournier nearly fifty years ago. One can almost feel Fournier's pride and satisfaction at the quality of the wines his "experimental" vines are producing today. They have an ample tasting room and a very welcoming atmosphere for anyone from the die-hard oenophile to the absolute beginner or the casual wine drinker. Tours of the vineyards and barrel rooms are easily arranged. They produce about 8,000 cases of wine per year.

Like many wineries, Standing Stone offers discounts and special events through various frequent-buyer programs. One of the more interesting twists is the Barrel Owners program, which entitles members to various complimentary wines over a five-year period and culminating in literal ownership of a now-exhausted oak wine barrel.

Ventosa Vineyards

Ventosa means "windy" in Italian, and everything from the name to the ambience of the tasting room to the heritage of the owner, Lenny Cecere, evokes Italy—including the wines. Ventosa's first vineyards were planted from 2000 to 2002, with the first vintage in 2002. The winery and tasting room opened in 2005.

Ventosa produces estate wines only from exclusively handpicked grapes. Most of their approximately 5,000 cases of wine produced each year are sold through the tasting room. The vineyards, which stretch behind the winery building at the north end of Seneca Lake, have twenty-three acres of vinifera only. A major focus here are the dry reds: Cabernet Franc, Cabernet Sauvignon, Pinot Noir, and the Italian varietal Sangiovese, a rare find in the Finger Lakes. The Finger Lakes–grown Sangiovese is a bit thinner-skinned than the Italian version, making a more delicate wine. Other reds include Lemberger and their Meritage blend Saggio (wise), combining Cab Franc, Cab Sauvignon, Merlot, and Syrah. The reds here are oak-aged anywhere from one to three years and spend at least a year in the cellar after bottling, so a newly released wine will be several years older than many other Finger Lakes reds. Whites include a Riesling, Chardonnay, Pinot Gris, and the very unusual Tocai Friulano—a fruit-forward Italian varietal reminiscent of Sauvignon Blanc and Pinot Grigio. Ventosa also produces unusual rosés, one from Lemberger, one from Sangiovese. On the dessert side is the rare—perhaps unique—ice wine from Tocai Friulano called Tocaice.

Winemaker Jenna LaVita is one of very few women winemakers in the region; she also oversees the vineyard. Her apprenticeship includes experience working with Fox Run winemaker Peter Bell and Shalestone's Rob Thomas. The emphasis here is on careful vineyard management (they thin out up to 40 percent of their fruit before *véraison*, or ripening), nuanced winemaking, and unusual and interesting varietals.

Villa Bellangelo Winery

The drive down to Villa Bellangelo's tasting room takes you past a few rows of what look like very old vines, and indeed the history of grape growing on this land goes back a long, long time by Finger Lakes standards. A mere thirty-five years after the Reverend William P. Bostwick got grapes going in Hammondsport in the early 1830s, a Dr. Robert

Dr. Spence's Concord vines at Villa Bellangelo, planted in 1866.

Spence planted these very Concord vines in 1866. Remaining here for heritage value rather than winemaking, these vines still produce grapes, but Bellangelo's history is much more recent.

The winery began in 1986 as Squaw Point Winery, producing native-grape and hybrid wines. In 2002 a new owner, Michael Litterio, renamed it Bellangelo and refocused the winery on vinifera wines. The current owners, Chris and Matthew Missick, acquired the winery in 2011 and have quickly established an excellent reputation for well-crafted wines.

Bellangelo emphasizes Riesling in white and Cab Franc in red. Vineyards (the winery does not have its own grapes except Dr. Spence's mentioned above) are exclusively Seneca Lake sourcings, including the familiar Sawmill Creek, Gibson, and Morris vineyards. (Bellangelo has excellent, and very detailed, information on their vineyard sources on their website, at www.bellangelo.com/pages/soils).

Wines here include Riesling, Chardonnay (oaked and un-oaked), Gewurz, Seyval Blanc, and a relatively rare (and pleasing) Moscato in the *frizzante* (slightly sparkling—a bit of fizz on the tongue) style. Reds include the Cab Franc, Pinot Noir, Merlot, and a Meritage blend in the classic Cab Sauv, Cab Franc, and Merlot combination. The reds tend to be aged, in oak and in the bottle, a bit longer than is customary in the region. Blends and a rosé round out the offerings. Dessert wines have a port and a very unusual *vin doux naturel* (VDN), a fortified wine made in this case with Muscat. A very popular wine in southern France, this is probably unique in the Finger Lakes—and delicious.

The winemaker at Villa Bellangelo is Nathan Kendall, who apprenticed at Ravines. Bellangelo produces in the region of 6,000 cases per year.

Owner Chris Missick is also the author of a sort of "winery autobiography" called *A Sense of Place,* which tells the Bellangelo story and is well worth reading. His treatment of Finger Lakes wine history is especially good, and Missick is an excellent writer.

Wagner Vineyards

Founded by longtime resident Bill Wagner in 1979, Wagner Vineyards is one of the larger and more tourist-oriented of the Finger Lakes wineries, while still producing excellent and nicely varied wines. Bill Wagner took early advantage of the passage of the Farm Winery Act in 1976, breaking ground on his winery soon after the act became law. He designed a distinctive octagonal building to be both tasting room (on the ground floor) and winery aging area (down below in the basement, where the underground space affords a consistently cool temperature). The building was up and running by June 1979, and Wagner has thrived there ever since. In the intervening years Wagner has added a restaurant, the Ginny Lee Cafe (named for

Bill Wagner breaks ground on Wagner Vineyards, just after passage of the 1976 Farm Winery Act.

Wagner's granddaughter and current manager of the restaurant, Ginny Lee), as well as a brewery, discussed below.

Wagner is one of the estate wineries in the Finger Lakes, meaning they sell wine made only from their own grapes. Their vineyards are extensive for the Finger Lakes, 250 acres, and produce an unusually wide variety of grapes, both vinifera and hybrids. Among the latter is a white-wine grape known as Melody, a Cornell-developed hybrid that Wagner vinifies as a varietal and produces a wine that is vaguely like Sauvignon Blanc. Wagner pioneered the growing of Melody, producing the first commercial planting in 1984. In addition Wagner grows and makes wine from all of the usual suspects including Riesling, Chardonnay, Gewürztraminer, Pinot Noir, Merlot, Cabernet Franc, Cabernet Sauvignon, Seyval Blanc, Vignoles, Vidal, Cayuga White, De Chaunac, Delaware, and Niagara, plus a few others for a remarkably diverse twenty different varieties. Other interesting wines at Wagner include three different ice wines, produced when nature allows, from Riesling, Vidal Blanc, and Vignoles, as well as a bottle-fermented sparkling Riesling. Their signature sweet blend is Alta B, named for Bill Wagner's mother, Alta Button.

Wagner's production runs to about 50,000 cases of wine per year, making it one of the larger producers of quality table wine.

Wagner's other distinction is beer, which can be sampled in the tasting room and is produced in an area just to the side of the winery. The brewery operation was launched in 1997. Although beyond the scope of this book, the Wagner microbrewery produces a popular line of craft beers in an impressive variety, including a Cherry Kölsch, a Maple Porter, a Triplebock Reserve, and many others, well worth sampling for the beer enthusiast.

Not to be missed on a trip to Wagner in the warmer months is the koi pond. The numerous fish here, accustomed to fish-food handouts from visitors (who can purchase bags of the stuff in the tasting room), rush to greet anyone who approaches the pond whether they have fish food or not. The roiling water comes alive with orange, black, and white fish.

Hermann J. Wiemer Vineyard

Hermann J. Wiemer Vineyard is rivalled only by Dr. Konstantin Frank Vinifera Wine Cellars for its long-standing commitment to producing among the finest wines in the Finger Lakes. Along with Dr. Frank and Walter S. Taylor, Hermann Wiemer stands as one of the key figures who helped to guide the Finger Lakes into the wine region we know today. Arriving in the US from his native Bernkastel, Germany in 1966, Wiemer brought with him extensive skill and knowledge of grafting and vine selection which enabled him, after years of effort, to cultivate vinifera vines that would thrive in the harsh winters of Central New York. Wiemer could see that if the problem of cold winters could be overcome by site selection and vine grafting, the soil—so like the rocky soil of his native Mosel region—could be enticed to yield wines as good as those from home. His success in this effort is one of the singular achievements in Finger Lakes winemaking.

Wiemer got his start in the Finger Lakes at the O-Neh-Dah Winery in Conesus, a producer of strictly sacramental wines, and soon moved on to work for Walter S. Taylor at Bully Hill Winery on Keuka Lake. As his familiarity with the Finger Lakes region grew, he became convinced that the best combination of soil and lake proximity lay a few miles east, on the western shore of Seneca Lake. Seneca is the deepest of the Finger Lakes and therefore the "lake effect" of temperature modulation is at its most benign. Wiemer found a parcel of 80 acres, which surrounds the winery today, and began planning to make his own wine.

These plans did not sit well with his employer, Walter S. Taylor, who during the holidays in December, 1980, when Wiemer was visiting family in Germany, sent him a telegram informing him his employment had been terminated ostensibly "due to financial problems" at Taylor. Wiemer was on his way. (Look for a copy of this famous telegram on the wall of the anteroom outside the Wiemer tasting room, just on the left as you enter.)

The original 80 acres of vines comprise what is today called the HJW Vineyard. Two other vineyards, north of the winery on Route 14, complete the Wiemer acreage. Most of the Josef Vineyard (named for his winemaker uncle), about 10 miles north, was planted with Riesling in 1977 by Wiemer when he was working for Bully Hill. (There was—and remains—a one-acre planting of Gewurztraminer, from 1967, the oldest Gewurz vines in the Finger Lakes.) Nearly twenty years later, in 1996, Wiemer was able to purchase this vineyard. The third parcel is known as the Magdalena Vineyard (named for Hermann's mother), just north of the Josef, comprising 24 acres in a location among the warmest in the Finger Lakes. The vines that inhabit Magdalena today were planted in 1999, with vines selected to take advantage of the disparate soils in the parcel.

These vineyards, varying in soils and micro-climates, have enabled Wiemer over the years to produce truly outstanding cool-climate wines. Wiemer wines are a very labor-intensive endeavor, using twenty-five different fermentation tanks to produce sometimes very small lots of wine from a particular part of a particular vineyard. Wines are fermented for various lengths, often four to five months, and aged as much as three years on the lees for their sparkling wines.

The winemaker today is co-owner Fred Merwath, who was Hermann Wiemer's long-time assistant until Wiemer retired from the business in 2007. Working alongside Merwath, focusing for the most part on operations, is Merwath's college friend and co-owner, Oskar Bynke.

Riesling is the signature wine at Wiemer, not surprising given Hermann's legacy, and they produce a wide range of dry, semi-dry, and dessert wines from the grape. Other whites include Chardonnay, Gruner Veltliner, and Gewürztraminer. Their reds are dominated by Cabernet Franc, with limited amounts (due to limited acreage) of Pinot Noir and Lemberger. Wiemer offers a vinifera blend, called their Cuvée Series, in a white, red and rosé. Their sparkling wines, all hand-riddled and hand-disgorged, have recently included a Cuvée blend of Chardonnay and Pinot Noir, a Blanc de blancs (all Chardonnay), a Blanc de noirs (all Pinot Noir), and a Brut Rosé. Dessert wines, produced in limited numbers from hand-selected grapes, are produced from Riesling and, unusual for Finger Lakes dessert wines, from Chardonnay and Sauvignon blanc.

Wiemer has won accolades in abundance from wine critics and at wine competitions. It is among very few Finger Lakes wineries aiming for a world-wide reputation and the quality of its wines back up these aspirations.

Ryan William Vineyard

Owner Ryan William came to the Finger Lakes from suburban Philadelphia in 2002, purchasing about forty acres of prime Banana Belt vineyard property on Norbud Road, just north of the present tasting room on Route 414 on Seneca Lake's eastern shoreline. About twenty of these acres are planted in vines, comprising vinifera only: Grüner Veltliner, Riesling, Gewürztraminer, Chardonnay, Pinot Noir, Merlot, and Cabernet

Franc. Most of the vineyard was planted between 2003 and 2007. At first he grew grapes only for sale to area wineries, which RWV still does, but he gradually began making wine, first doing small-lot experiments for other wineries, then starting to vinify the fruit on his own.

Careful vineyard management is the watchword here, and the excellent estate wines William produces bear out the effectiveness of his efforts. His wines are meant to show the character of the fruit, not the inventiveness of the winemaker. He strives to keep the process of winemaking as simple as possible: "Wine is grapes and yeast," he says. "The wine should be a vessel for the fruit." The vineyard is the most important element of his winery, and he devotes great care to it. Alternating rows are planted with ryegrass, for example, to break up the compaction of the soil and improve vine health. He has experimented with different trellising methods, making wine in two batches from different trellis systems, to judge the results.

The tasting room at Ryan William is a restored 1865 barn.

He is looking for maturity in his fruit, which is more than simple ripeness. It is a balance of acidity and flavor, producing wines that are fresh and not heavy. He makes decisions on when to harvest based strictly on taste. While he knows the brix and pH levels of his grapes, numbers do not drive his harvest decisions.

Ryan William produces varietal wines of each of the grapes grown in the vineyard. Riesling is typically picked three times to produce dry, less dry, and late-harvest wines. The winery sometimes produces a rosé, using the Pinot Noir or the Cab Franc.

The newly completed tasting room on Route 414 is the culmination of a three-year project restoring a barn that was originally across the road (remnants of which are still visible). This barn dates from about 1865 and was dismantled and reconstructed with new walls and a new interior. The beams and basic construction are all original. Along the top of the structure run single beams seventy-two feet in length. The stone foundation wall from the original barn surrounds the new, although the new building rests on a concrete foundation.

Ryan William also raises beef cattle, some pastured behind the tasting room and some on Norbud Road. This project was the result of his wish to maintain a closer connection to the land and the food it produces. The cattle are also an excellent, natural way to clear pastureland—slower but more in tune with Nature than using a bulldozer.

These are high-quality wines made with fruit grown with great care. Ryan William produces about 1,200 cases per year.

Zugibe Vineyards

Zugibe Vineyards (it's pronounced (*ZUGG-a-bee*) is the happy result of owner Fred Zugibe III deciding not to follow in the footsteps of his father and grandfather to become a physician. Instead he started a vineyard in 2005 with twenty-three acres of vinifera wine grapes, which has since grown to forty acres planted with eleven vinifera varietals: Riesling, Gewürztraminer, Pinot Gris, Chardonnay, Sauvignon Blanc, and Grüner Veltliner in the whites, and Cabernet Franc, Cabernet Sauvignon, Pinot Noir, Merlot, and Lemberger in the reds. Wines are 100 percent estate wines; their first released vintage was in 2009.

Zugibe's focus is on dry wines: Whites are Grüner Veltliner (they are one of the first producers of GV in the Finger Lakes), Pinot Gris, a dry Gewürztraminer, Chardonnay, and Riesling. Reds are a Pinot Noir, Cab Franc, and the Meritage "4 Freds Red," a nice blend of Merlot, the two Cabs, and Lemberger, and named for Fred's forebears as well as his son, Freddie. Sweeter wines are the Firebird White, which blends vinifera with Vignoles, and Firebird Blush, a blend with Aurore.

Fred's late father, Fred Zugibe Jr., a prominent heart specialist, designed the Z-shield logo on their labels; when he died the image of the phoenix was added to encircle it as a tribute to his memory. Other Zugibes in the business include Fred's brothers Sean, who manages the vineyard, and Brendan, who works with their wholesaler in distribution of the wines.

The Zugibe Kitchen is an on-site restaurant that specializes in Zugibe-heritage Lebanese cuisine. Unfortunately not open at the time of my wintertime tasting visit, the restaurant has very nice reviews. And how often do you get good Lebanese cuisine on the shores of Seneca Lake?

Zugibe produces about 5,000 cases per year.

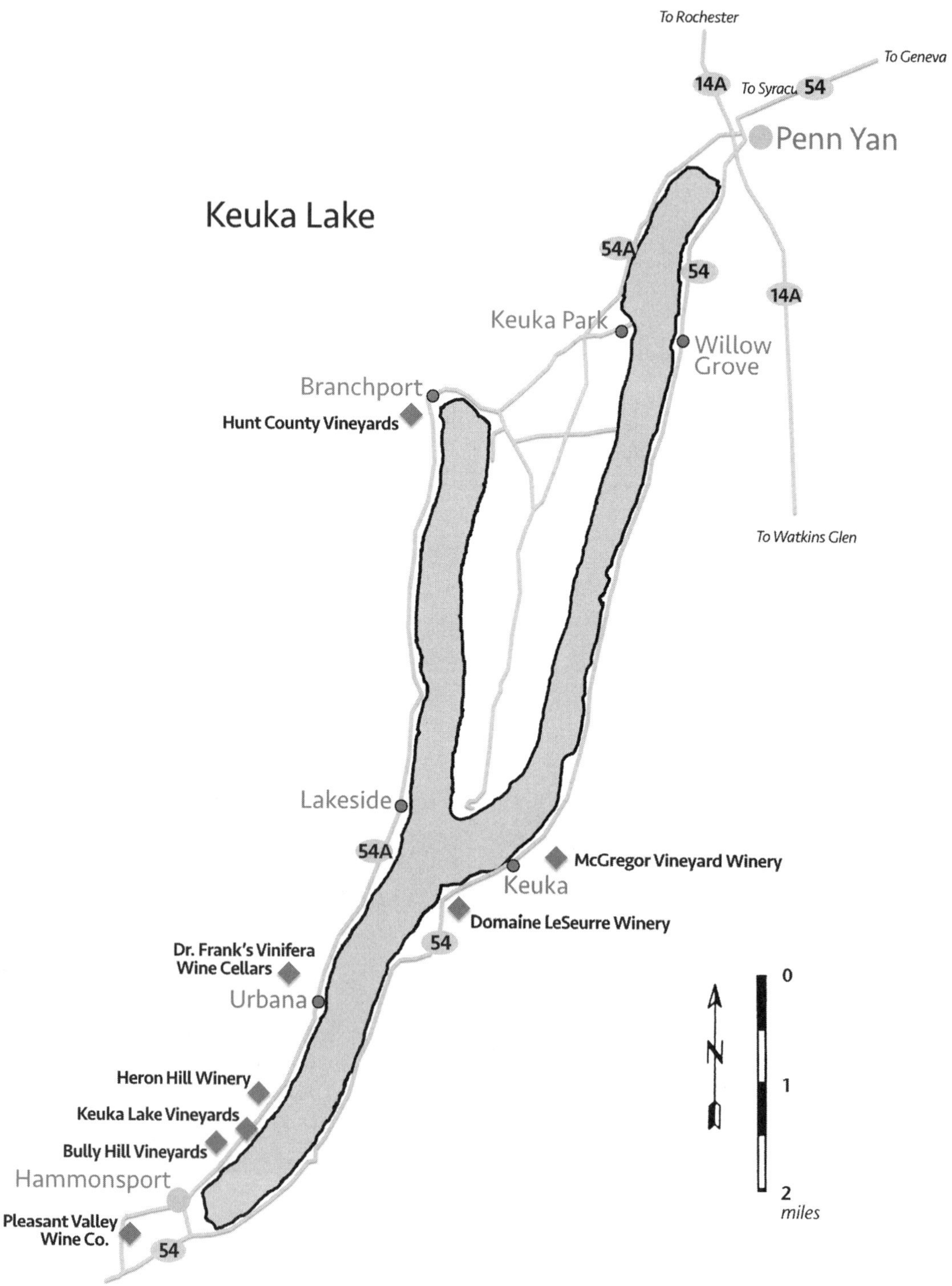
Keuka Lake
To Rochester
To Geneva
14A
To Syracu
54
Penn Yan
54A
54
14A
Keuka Park
Willow Grove
Branchport
Hunt County Vineyards
To Watkins Glen
Lakeside
54A
McGregor Vineyard Winery
Keuka
Domaine LeSeurre Winery
54
Dr. Frank's Vinifera Wine Cellars
Urbana
Heron Hill Winery
Keuka Lake Vineyards
Bully Hill Vineyards
Hammonsport
Pleasant Valley Wine Co.
54
N
0
1
2
miles

3 | *Keuka Lake Wineries*

KEUKA LAKE is of course where the Finger Lakes wine story began, with Reverend Bostwick's small vineyard in Hammondsport. It is also home to many of the important milestones of Finger Lakes wine history, from the first commercial winery in Pleasant Valley Wine Company, to the rise of the Taylor Wine Company and Gold Seal, the emergence of Bully Hill Vineyards under the colorful Walter S. Taylor, and the founding of Dr. Konstantin Frank Vinifera Wine Cellars. Today some of these famous wineries still make wine on Keuka Lake, but are joined by interesting newcomers such as Domaine LeSeurre and Keuka Lake Vineyards. Although not as numerous as the wineries on Seneca Lake, the Keuka wineries offer a rich variety of history and winemaking styles.

Bully Hill Vineyards

Bully Hill Vineyards is the legacy of the infectiously flamboyant Walter S. Taylor, one of the Finger Lakes wine world's most interesting and influential characters. As discussed previously, Taylor started Bully Hill shortly before being fired by his family's Taylor Wine Company in 1970, joining a list of prestigious Finger Lakes winemakers whose dismissal prompted the flourishing of new wineries. Like Konstantin Frank, Walter S. Taylor wanted to make quality wine and was dismayed by the profit-at-all-costs posture of the major Finger Lakes wine producers, Taylor included. His outspoken expression of this opinion led to his ouster from Taylor, which permitted him to exert all his energy on his recently founded new winery, Bully Hill on the western slopes of

Keuka Lake, just north of Hammondsport, on land that was the original home of the Taylor Wine Company when it was established by Walter S. Taylor's grandfather in 1882. Taylor waged a celebrated feud with the Coca-Cola Company (see part 1), in which lawyers for Coca-Cola, which had purchased Taylor Wine Co. in 1977, filed injunctions against Taylor's using his name in conjunction with his new winery. The dispute lives on in labels and signs with name Taylor blacked out. Several such signs are visible today at Bully Hill.

Bully Hill is arguably the most enthusiastically commercial of the Finger Lakes wineries, a characteristic that no doubt stems from Walter S. Taylor's instincts for showmanship. Bully Hill sponsors NASCAR racers, hockey teams, and more, its logo pasted on cars and jerseys—it is even the "official wine" of the Boston Red Sox. This situation might lead one to anticipate a theme-park sort of experience at the winery, but by pleasant contrast the winery building and tasting room is a polished, understated affair, with a restaurant overlooking the vineyards and lake, two tasting rooms (one offers a set "menu" of wines; the other has virtually all the Bully Hill wines available for a self-selected tasting), and the modest but interesting Greyton H. Taylor Wine Museum. This is well worth a visit and features objects and photographs from the early years of Finger Lakes winemaking, back to the mid-nineteenth century and beyond. Adjunct to the museum is the Walter S. Taylor Art Gallery, featuring the founder's paintings, including many of his labels. Off to the back of the tasting room, have a look into the vineyard and you'll see Taylor's famous pink railroad tank car, the vestige of one of his many publicity stunts. Taylor had the car rolled into the property to showcase his charge that the big-time Finger Lakes wines producers were adulterating their wines with cheap California juice ostensibly delivered by tank car in the dead of night.

The entrance to the Walter S. Taylor Art Gallery with the name "Taylor" redacted.

Taylor's famous tank car, towed into the vineyard as a publicity stunt to tweak larger wineries for their use of "shipped in" California juice.

Bully Hill offers much of the standard list of Riesling, Chardonnay, Pinot Noir, and others, but also has an interesting selection of rare hybrids not often made into varietals, including St. Croix, Marechal Foch, Ravat 51, and Verdelet. Bully Hill wines feature quirky but appealing labels, many of which were drawn or painted by Walter S. Taylor himself. Walter Taylor died in 2001. The winery today is run by Taylor's wife,

Lillian Taylor, making Bully Hill, like so many Finger Lakes wineries, a family business of long standing.

Grapes from Bully Hill wines come from their own vineyards and from other grape growers in the region. There remain a few vines from the original Taylor Wine Co. of the 1800s, still growing on the slope just below the tasting room.

Bully Hill's wines are deliberately un-fussy, and they offer a wide-ranging selection of vinifera and sometimes rare hybrids that are well worth sampling. As the embodiment of a significant piece of Finger Lakes wine history, Bully Hill is an important winery to get to know.

Domaine LeSeurre Winery

Everything about Domaine LeSeurre has a French flavor, from the labels on certain bottles that say "Élevé en Fût de Chêne Français" (that's "aged in French oak barrels") right down to the signs in the parking lot that proclaim "Stationnement" with a helpful "Parking" beneath it. In a wine region sometimes dominated by Riesling and comparisons to the great wine districts of Germany, Domaine LeSeurre has proudly planted the *tricolore* of France on the shores of Keuka Lake. And a welcome addition it is.

Owners Sébastien and Céline LeSeurre are a young couple with a deep history in winemaking. For Sébastien that means five generations of his family before him have been professional winemakers in the Champagne district of northeastern France. Céline, originally from Toulouse, grew up tramping the vineyards belonging to her grandparents near the French Pyrenees. Both have a deep knowledge and love for wine, cultivated in winemaking study and practice in France, Australia, and New Zealand, where they met in 2009.

In 2011 they arrived in the Finger Lakes, loved the area, and recognized the region's potential for outstanding wines. Their first vintage was in 2012, and their tasting room opened in 2013. The tasting room, a few miles north of Hammondsport on Keuka's eastern shore, is surrounded by about eight acres of what will soon be vineyards. Until the planting happens they source grapes from six carefully selected vineyards that they lease on Keuka, Seneca, and Cayuga Lakes. "Carefully" selected is understating it: They tasted grapes from some four hundred vineyards before settling on these six. And for now, the actual winemaking is done at a facility on Cayuga Lake, until they can ramp up their own winery on their Keuka Lake land.

As winemakers they take exceptional care: Clearly Domaine LeSeurre is out to make the best possible wine, not the most. They age their Barrel Select Riesling for twelve months (one of very, very few Finger Lakes wineries to age Riesling in oak). Their Cuvée series of Riesling is aged nine months in stainless-steel tanks.

Currently their offerings include Chardonnay, Riesling, and Gewürztraminer in the whites, and Pinot Noir and Cab Franc in the reds. They have a Cabernet Franc rosé as well. The wines are grouped between oak-aged (called Barrel Select) and stainless-steel (called Cuvée). Their whites are all stirred on the lees (*bâtonnage*) to soften acidity and reduce tartness, especially in the Rieslings. Oak aging is seriously handcrafted as well, with Chardonnay and Cabernet Franc oaked separately in new barrels, used barrels, and neutral barrels and then combined to suit the winemaker's goals.

These are clearly serious winemakers, and although Domaine LeSeurre remains in only its first few vintages, this is a winery to watch carefully.

Looking for Domaine LeSeurre wines at a wine store will get you nowhere, at least for now. Handcrafted wines such as these are produced in very small quantities, even by the relatively modest standards of the Finger Lakes. Their wines can be purchased only at the tasting room, or online at their website.

Everything about Domaine LeSeurre bespeaks France . . .

Dr. Konstantin Frank Vinifera Wine Cellars

The legend of Dr. Konstantin Frank has been told many times and in many places, this book included (see page 36). It is a story well worth hearing, for it's safe to say that without Dr. Frank, there would probably be none of the Finger Lakes wines, or wineries, that we enjoy today. As noted earlier, Konstantin Frank was the first, and by far the most vocal, proponent of traditional vinifera wines in the Finger Lakes, arguing that anything less was unworthy of a winemaker's efforts. Prior to Dr. Frank, even ambitious, respected, talented winemakers like Charles Fournier believed that the region could not be a reliable home to the classic vinifera varieties such as Chardonnay, Cabernet Franc, and all the rest—it was simply too cold. The region, they believed, would have to make do with, at best, the hybrid wines such as Seyval Blanc that were better suited to the climate here, with vinifera being possible only some of the time, when winemakers got lucky.

Dr. Frank proved them wrong. Arriving in the United States from his native Ukraine in 1952, Frank sought out Gold Seal president Charles Fournier and convinced him that vinifera wines could be made in the Finger Lakes. He had such confidence because the climate in Ukraine and Russia, where he had successfully grown vinifera, was so much like that of the Finger Lakes. Fournier hired Dr. Frank, who began planting grapes.

After years of exhaustive experimentation, Frank had succeeded. But conflicts with the executives at Gold Seal over the future of hybrids there led Dr. Frank to leave and start his own winery in 1962. There it remains today, surrounded by vineyards planted by Dr. Frank himself, and having become the winery perhaps best known internationally for quality wine made in the Finger Lakes.

Today the winery is still run by the descendants of Konstantin Frank. Dr. Frank's son Willy Frank took over management of the winery in 1984 and expanded the range and reputation of Dr. Frank wines. Among his many accomplishments was the introduction of a sparkling-wine label,

Chateau Frank, in the late 1980s. The Chateau Frank wines are made strictly in the *méthode champenoise* fashion, and from the grapes traditionally used to make "genuine" French champagne: Chardonnay, Pinot Noir, and Pinot Meunier. (These wines are made in a separate building, the unassuming stone structure just down the road from the Dr. Frank winery.) Willy Frank was succeeded by his son Fred Frank, who runs the winery today and was responsible for adding the value-wine label, Salmon Run. Fred's daughter Meghan Frank is general manager and next in line.

The vineyards at Dr. Frank comprise about sixty acres that surround the winery, and include plantings of Cabernet Sauvignon from the late 1950s, the oldest Cab Sauv vines east of the Rockies and of course virtually antique by Finger Lakes standards. The Dr. Frank planting of Grüner Veltliner, at ten acres, is the largest outside of Austria. Also from the 1950s is a planting of a rare white-wine grape, Rkatsiteli (pronounced *arr-katz-e-TELL-y*), which originated in the republic of Georgia in the Caucasus, near Dr. Frank's native Ukraine. The winery's Pinot Noir vines are also veterans—the second-oldest Pinot Noir in the United States. In addition to these, other Dr. Frank–owned vineyards are spread throughout the Finger Lakes region, totaling around two hundred acres. All fruit for the Dr. Konstantin Frank wines come from Dr. Frank vineyards. (The Salmon Run label sources from other area vineyards, as is the case for limited amounts of grapes for the Chateau Frank sparkling wines.) The vineyard manager, Eric Volz, is also a member of the Frank family—Dr. Frank was his grandfather.

Dr. Frank Wine Cellars has won awards in abundance; these are uniformly well-made wines. The whites include most of the vinifera wines one finds throughout the Finger Lakes—Riesling, of course, as well as Chardonnay, Pinot Gris, Sauvignon Blanc, Grüner Veltliner, and Gewürztraminer. In addition there are somewhat rarer wines—Muscat Ottonel, Pinot Blanc, and rarest of all in the whites, Rkatsiteli. The reds echo the same theme, with some more or less expected wines such as the two Cabs (Sauvignon and Franc), Pinot Noir, Lemberger, Merlot, and a Meritage, plus some outliers—in this case, a Saperavi (also found at McGregor and Standing Stone), which is a rich, earthy red that is attracting more attention among Finger Lakes winemakers—the word means "painted" in the language of the republic of Georgia. Rarest of all is a red that Dr. Frank's calls Cuvée d'Amour, a kind of super-Tuscan-style red made in this case from a grape called *Vitis amurensis,* from the Amur River Valley in southern Siberia. This grape makes an excellent wine and, unlike a Sangiovese that might go into a Super Tuscan, can withstand winter temperatures as low as thirty below Fahrenheit. This offering is unique in the Finger Lakes, at least for now.

The Chateau Frank sparkling wines are also excellent and include a blanc de noirs (made from Pinot Noir and Pinot Meunier), a blanc de blancs (all Chardonnay), a brut, and a rosé sparkler.

One recent and very appealing initiative was launched by Meghan Frank and involves single-vineyard Rieslings, named for two important women in the Dr. Frank family: Eugenia, Dr. Frank's wife, was Meghan Frank's great-grandmother; her namesake wine is a stainless-steel-fermented Riesling. Margaret was Willy Frank's wife, Meghan's grandmother; this wine is oak-fermented. Both are made in small lots of about fifty cases each.

Dr. Frank's has six winemakers to cover the range and volume of their production, which is large for the region—somewhere north of 70,000 cases per year.

Heron Hill Winery

Heron Hill gets its name from the favorite bird of co-owner Josephine Ingle, the blue heron. Josephine and John Ingle first planted vines on their twenty acres of Canandaigua Lake property in 1972, in all some twelve thousand vines of Chardonnay, Riesling and Seyval Blanc, with the goal of selling grapes to area wineries. A few years later, when the vines had matured and were producing grapes, the market had turned against them and they were left with little choice for their crops but to open a winery. It was a happy problem.

From these hardworking early days the Ingles have built one of the most successful and interesting wineries in the Finger Lakes, home to a beautiful tasting room and excellent wines. The Ingles decided to locate the winery near successful neighbors Dr. Konstantin Frank and Bully Hill on the western side of Keuka Lake. Their first vintage was in 1977—very early days for Finger Lakes winemaking. The original Ingle Vineyard on Canandaigua Lake continues to provide fruit for Heron Hill, along with about twelve acres that stretch in front of the tasting room, on the south side of the access road. Other grapes, such as those used in their single-vineyard Riesling series, are sourced from select vineyards throughout the Finger Lakes.

Riesling is an important varietal at Heron Hill, and they showcase the wine with a very illuminating series of single-vineyard wines sourced from five different Finger Lakes. The labels for the series portray a hand, with the outlines of the five lakes superimposed over it. The goal is to

take fruit from five different vineyards and treat each the same in the winemaking process, in order to display the distinctions in the terroir from one vineyard to the next. Five unique microclimates result in five different wines. The five lakes and their vineyards are Canandaigua (Ingle Vineyard, the original); Keuka (Heron Hill, the vineyard in front of the winery); Seneca (Morris Vineyard); Cayuga (Patrician Verona Vineyard, at Hosmer Winery); and Skaneateles (Hobbit Hollow Farm). The Ingle Vineyard wine has been a separate single-vineyard Riesling since the late 1980s, predating the current emphasis on single-vineyard winemaking by many years.

The tasting room at Heron Hill, named one of the top 100 tasting rooms in the world.

In addition to these and other Rieslings, Heron Hill offers Chardonnay, Gewurz, Valvin Muscat, and some blends. Reds include Pinot Noir, Baco Noir, Cab Franc, Merlot, and a Meritage blend of classic Bordeaux varieties Cabernet Franc, Merlot, and Cabernet Sauvignon called The Chosen Spot. On the dessert side they have late-harvest Vidal Blanc, LH Riesling, and Riesling ice wine when possible.

The tasting room at Heron Hill is not to be missed: Its huge vaulted ceilings evoke the interior of a wine barrel. Built in 2000 along with the accompanying restaurant, the tasting room was named one of the ten most spectacular in the world by *Travel + Leisure* magazine. Only two were selected in the United States: Heron Hill, and Opus One in California's Napa Valley. (It is worth noting that Opus One is open only by appointment, and a tasting there will run roughly ten times the cost of a tasting at Heron Hill. Yet another reason to come to the Finger Lakes!)

Heron Hill produces roughly 20,000 cases of wine per year.

Hunt Country Vineyards

Hunt Country Vineyards in Branchport, at the top of the western branch of Keuka Lake, began when owners Art and Joyce Hunt moved to a 170-acre farm, which had belonged to Art's grandfather, in 1973. They decided to grow grapes for sale to the then-major wineries in the region. When Taylor, a significant customer, was acquired by Coca-Cola (covered earlier in this book in part 1), the market for the Hunts' grapes vanished as the winemaking was moved to California. Fortunately for the Hunts, the Farm Winery Act was passed and in 1981 they formed Finger Lakes Wine Cellars as a small-scale winery. As the business built up steam they renamed it Hunt Country Vineyards in 1987. The Hunts have been very active in the Finger Lakes wine industry: Joyce is a founding member and past president of the Keuka Lake Wine Trail, and Art and Joyce received the Unity Award in 1999 from the New York Wine and Grape Foundation for their efforts to promote unity among producers in the industry.

Today the winery is managed by Jonathan Hunt, son of Art and Joyce and the sixth generation of Hunts to farm this acreage. The winemaker is Brian Barry. Hunt Country grows fourteen varieties of grapes on forty-eight acres surrounding the winery, including vinifera (Cab Franc, Chardonnay, and Riesling); various hybrids, including the rather rare Chambourcin, Corot Noir, and De Chaunac; and three native-grape varieties, Catawba, Concord, and Niagara. About three-quarters of their fruit goes into Hunt Country wine; the remainder is sold to area wineries. Occasionally they source from other New York State growers, including North Fork (Long Island) producers, especially if they are in need of additional grapes for vinifera reds. Harvesting is done both by hand and by machine, depending upon the condition of the grapes and the needs of the winemaker.

Estate wines include the Cabernet Franc, Chardonnay, Riesling, and all the hybrids. In dry wines they offer mostly whites, including an oaked

Chardonnay (an un-oaked Chardonnay is on the horizon), dry and semi-dry Riesling, Vidal Blanc, and Seyval Blanc, and a blanc de blancs (all Chardonnay) sparkling wine. Blends include a Chablis-style wine called Pearl, combining Chardonnay, Pinot Gris, and Cayuga White. Despite this their best-selling wine is a dry red, a nice blend of Cab Franc, Lemberger, Merlot, and Cab Sauv called Alchemy. One of their specialties is ice wine—Hunt Country is the oldest continuous producer of ice wine in the Finger Lakes, their first vintage dating to 1987. Typically their ice wine is from Vidal Blanc.

Other notable wines include a Valvin Muscat in a semi-dry style and a Dolce di Moscato, much sweeter at 5 percent RS. Upcoming will be a late-harvest Vidal Blanc, which will join their other dessert wines, a fortified cream sherry and a late-harvest Vignoles.

They also offer a sweet Niagara white called Foxy Lady and a blush, Sweet Gus, named for their late dog, with a portion of the sale donated in Gus's name to the Humane Society.

The Hunts' daughter Suzanne is active in the sustainable-energy field and has led an effort to bring solar energy to Hunt Country as well as other area wineries including Wagner, Dr. Frank, Eagle Crest, and Lakewood. The solar panels at Hunt Country are designed to supply about 75 percent of their electricity needs (the vagaries of the local utility company got in the way of going 100 percent solar).

Hunt Country Vineyards produces about 10,000 cases of wine annually.

Keuka Lake Vineyards

Mel Goldman, the owner and vineyard manager of Keuka Lake Vineyards, began his life in the Finger Lakes the way many people do—coming for a visit (in his case visiting Cornell with his soon-to-be-college-aged son) and falling in love with the region. Goldman took his fondness for the Finger Lakes one significant step further, deciding to pursue his lifelong dream of owning a farm by purchasing vineyard land that

had belonged to Taylor on Keuka Lake. Goldman took early retirement and, in 1997, Keuka Lake Vineyards was born.

At first the vineyards were just that—Goldman planted Riesling and Pinot Noir and sold his entire crop to area wineries. This continued for several years until the winemaking urge became impossible to resist. Starting as a home winemaker, with batches for family and friends, Goldman increased his knowledge and abilities under the tutelage of Ravines owner and winemaker Morten Hallgren and in 2005 released his first Keuka Lake Vineyards wine. Goldman has since passed the winemaking reins to the current winemaker, Katey Larwood.

Keuka Lake Vineyards has land on both sides of the lake, totaling about fifty-two acres. Part of their holdings surround the winery and tasting room on Route 76 north of Hammondsport. Other acreage is on the east side of Keuka Lake, on land planted in the early 1950s by the legendary Charles Fournier. (Some of the Fournier-planted vines remain in the form of Leon Millot grapes, which Keuka Lake vinifies as a varietal.)

KLV wines are almost all estate (from grapes grown in their own vineyards), with some Cab Franc and Vignoles sourced from other Finger Lake vineyards. The specialties are Riesling, Vignoles, and Cabernet Franc, plus the Leon Millot mentioned above. Millot is a red hybrid and close cousin to Marechal Foch, and although hybrids in general are quite common here, Millot is a rarity—this is one of very few varietal Leon Millot wines in the Finger Lakes. The KLV Rieslings are done in single-vineyard offerings in dry style, plus a semi-dry. Vignoles, again a common grape yet somehow not a common varietal wine, is made "gently dry" and as an orange wine, with skin contact similar to red-wine-making technique. KLV makes the "orange" Vignoles when the quality of the fruit supports it and typically leaves the wine on the skins for ten to fourteen days. Cab Franc is also vinified as a varietal. Other wines are blends: Tin Pathi, a white blend of Chardonnay, Vignoles, and Riesling, gets its name from a Nepalese card game—owner Mel Goldman was in the Peace Corps in Nepal. Their KLV Red is a dry blend of Cab Franc, Leon Millot, and Pinot Noir.

On the sweet side is a Delaware, an old-fashioned native labrusca red wine, with typically foxy character. They also have a low-alcohol port-style red called Hammondsport.

Keuka Lake Vineyards strives for careful, hand-tended vineyard management using sustainable methods. The winemaking philosophy is to employ minimal intervention and let the wines express the quality of the soil, the vineyard siting, and the microclimates. Winemaker Katey Larwood is a California-bred winemaker with a love of Riesling, which brought her to the Finger Lakes. Like many winemakers she is always willing to try something new, such as the orange Vignoles mentioned above, or the recent experiment with Leon Millot Nouveau, produced by fermenting on the skins for four days, pressing the wine, finishing fermentation in tanks, and then a quick month of oak aging before bottling, only forty-eight days from picking.

"Harvest Day" at Keuka Lake Vineyards, when winelovers can try harvesting some Riesling.

Wine lovers who have always wanted to get their boots muddy—and learn what vineyard work is like—can indulge themselves by signing up for KLV's Riesling Harvest Day. Volunteers show up at the winery in the morning, take up a pair of pruning shears, and (after some instruction) spend the day picking Riesling. The reward is a bountiful dinner at day's end. Details are on KLV's website.

Keuka Lake Vineyards is relatively small, at about 3,500 cases per year, but it has won awards and acclaim in abundance and is proud to have its wines served in sixty-five restaurants in the hypercompetitive world of New York City wine lists.

McGregor Vineyard

Owners Bob and Marge McGregor began planting vinifera and hybrid grapes on their twenty-eight acres overlooking Keuka Lake in 1971—virtually the Stone Age for vinifera-grape growing in the Finger Lakes. Their early confidence in the ability of vinifera to survive the cold has been rewarded with wines that are among the best-regarded in the Finger Lakes, especially their reds.

The winery itself had its first vintage in 1980, with Chardonnay, Riesling, Gewurz, and Pinot Noir. Over the years they have increased plantings substantially with red vinifera Cab Franc, Cab Sauvignon, Merlot, Pinot Noir, and even Sangiovese. Vinifera whites are Chardonnay, Riesling, Muscat Ottonel, and Gewurz, with hybrids Cayuga White and Vignoles. Of particular interest are some grapes from Russia, Ukraine, and the Caucasus: Saperavi, which is also produced at Dr. Frank and

Standing Stone but few if any others in the region; Rkatsiteli, a white-wine grape (also at Dr. Frank), and Sereksiya Charni, a very obscure red-wine grape from Ukraine. McGregor may be the only winery outside the Caucasus that produces this wine.

White wines at McGregor include Chardonnay, Riesling, Gewurz, and Muscat Ottonel. They have a rosé of both Pinot Noir and Cab Franc, and a blush-wine blend of equal quantities of Rkatsiteli and Sereksiya. On the red side McGregor has varietals of Cab Sauv, Cab Franc, and Pinot Noir, and they are renowned for two red blends, Rob Roy and Black Russian. Rob Roy is a blend of the two Cabs and Merlot, made richer by oaking twice. The wines are made first as varietals and oaked in that process, then blended and oak-aged again. Black Russian Red is a "field blend" of Saperavi and Sereksiya Charni, meaning the harvested grapes go together into the picking crate and are vinified together from there. The vines for these grapes originated from vines brought by Dr. Frank in the 1950s, coming to Bob McGregor via Dr. John McGrew of the USDA. The vines were planted in 1980, and originally McGregor produced these as single-grape varietals. In 1991 they decided to try them blended together—and the results were splendid. Each year they make Black Russian Red which ages very well (bottles in the winery library are twenty-five years old and still evolving).

McGregor's Black Russian Red

McGregor is managed on a day-to-day basis by John McGregor, the son of the founders. The winemaker is Jeff Dencenburg.

These are all excellent, carefully crafted wines from top-quality fruit, but the red-wine drinker in particular should be sure to put McGregor on the tasting list. The tasting room, by the way, has a nice twist. Instead of the typical tasting bar, McGregor has tasters sit a picnic tables both indoors and out, and they bring the wines to you—along with a small plate of nibbles (crackers, cheese, chocolates) to try with the wines.

McGregor is 100 percent estate wine for the vinifera; hybrids are sourced from other Keuka Lake vineyards. Case quantity is about 5,000.

Pleasant Valley Wine Company

Wines at Pleasant Valley tend more toward the taste of a sweet-tooth wine consumer, but a visit here is really a must-see for the student of Finger Lakes wines, because this is where it all began. Established in 1860, Pleasant Valley remains US Bonded Winery #1, and although much has changed, of course, much also remains, including the stone buildings from the original winery that are still used today in making wine.

The scale of winemaking at Pleasant Valley is unlike anything else in the Finger Lakes, with the exception of what is now Hazlitt's Red Cat production facility in Naples. The large, cubical building next to the present tasting room is their press building—a building devoted entirely to pressing. Most Finger Lakes wineries will have a room, or part of a room, for pressing. The pipes that run across the road carry juice from the press building up to the winery—there are about twenty-three miles of wine-pipe here in all. While the scale may feel industrial, it's worth noting that most wine, even very good wine, is produced in what looks more like a factory than a craft studio. Major California producers, for example, have wineries that are in line with the size and scope of Pleasant Valley. The winemaking, as noted, is done across the road, in the original buildings; aging is done in caves carved into the hillside in the nineteenth century.

The press building at Pleasant Valley Wine Company, with wine-pipe on girders running across the road.

At Pleasant Valley, too, the legacy labels of the early years of Finger Lakes winemaking have been collected together after many years of separation. Here one can sample wines labeled not only Pleasant Valley but also Gold Seal, Great Western, and Widmer. The history of these brands (discussed in part 1) is fairly involved, but the crux of the matter is that Pleasant Valley owner Mike Doyle, whose family purchased the company in 1995, has over the years acquired the rights to these iconic wine labels as well.

The Doyle family is also active in Finger Lakes vineyards—Matt Doyle, Mike Doyle's son, is the owner of Doyle Vineyard Management, which sells grapes and performs a variety of vineyard-management duties for many wineries throughout the region. Many of the wines made at Pleasant Valley are sourced from these Doyle vineyards. They include the largest plantings of Chardonnay and Riesling in the eastern United States.

Probably the most famous brand here is Great Western, the American champagne that is still produced. How the "classic" Great Western Champagne differed from today's product can never be known for sure, although speculation is that it ran somewhat sweeter, perhaps with more native-grape wine added, than the wine today. Great Western Champagne today is a blend of Chardonnay, Catawba, and Delaware. More traditional is the Millennium Brut Champagne, made of 100 percent Chardonnay. Various other sparkling wines tend more toward native-grape varieties and are sweeter, as are the Widmer and Gold Seal wines. The best seller is the very sweet Chocolate Lab, the "Lab" being for "labrusca"—with chocolate added. The label features the sort of chocolate Lab we might think of first, a puppy face to melt the heart of even a cat lover. Also in the dessert category is a very nice solera dry sherry, produced in the traditional solera method and aged in oak from four to six years, and made from Chardonnay and some labrusca fruit.

Pleasant Valley's importance in the Finger Lakes wine world owes much to its history, but the wines deserve a try even for the dry-vinifera devotee.

Bibliography

Baxevanis, John J. *The Wine Regions of America.* Stroudsburg, PA: Vinifera Wine Growers Journal, 1992.

Cattell, Hudson. *Wines of Eastern North America.* Ithaca, NY: Cornell University Press, 2014.

Dawson, Evan. *Summer in a Glass.* New York: Sterling, 2011.

Figiel, Richard. *Circle of Vines.* Albany, NY: SUNY Press, 2014.

————. *Culture in a Glass.* Lodi, NY: Silver Thread Books, 1995.

Goode, Jamie. *The Science of Wine.* Berkeley: University of California Press, 2014.

Halliday, James and Hugh Johnson. *The Art and Science of Wine.* London: Mitchell-Beazley, 1992.

Hartsock, John C. *Seasons of a Finger Lakes Winery.* Ithaca, NY: Cornell University Press, 2011.

Pellechia, Thomas. *Over a Barrel.* Albany, NY: SUNY Press, 2015.

Pinney, Thomas. *A History of Wine in America.* Berkeley: University of California Press, 1989, 2005.

Robinson, Jancis. *Vines, Grapes and Wines.* London: Mitchell-Beazley, 1986.

Winemaster: the Dr. Konstantin Frank Story. Amsterdam NY: Noteworthy Co., 1983.

Index